Why We Think The Way We Do And How To Change It

Thomas Garvey and Dr Helen Kogan

Clink Street

London | New York

Published by Clink Street Publishing 2017

Copyright © 2017

First edition.

ISBN: 978-1-911525-43-1 paperback
ISBN: 978-1-911525-44-8 ebook

Thomas Garvey's relationship with *The Science of Acting* began in 1987 when he was taught by Sam Kogan at the London drama school that Thomas was then attending. The integrity, inspiration and dedication Sam demonstrated towards his work never left him, and upon hearing Sam had opened his own school (the then *School of The Science of Acting*) Thomas put his career on hold to study with him for 4 years. This was a period where *The Science of Acting* was rapidly evolving, with the subjects developing class by class. During Thomas' 30-year Theatre career he has been an actor, director, producer and teacher. He has been teaching *The Science of Acting* for over 15 years which includes being a Senior Acting Tutor at *The Kogan Academy of Dramatic Art* and its Head of Directing for 5 years.

Thomas now runs his own Personal Development Company.

Dr Helen Kogan has had a lifelong interest in exploring the nature of consciousness. Initially pursuing the path of scientific investigation, Helen followed her first degree in Neuroscience with a Doctorate in Neuropharmacology. After her father's death in 2004, Helen temporarily took the role of Principal at *The Kogan Academy of Dramatic Arts* and remained Chair of the board for a subsequent decade, during which time she compiled and edited *The Science of Acting* (Routeledge, 2009). Ever-since Helen has been travelling the world. Having (at the time of writing) visited close to 90 countries, she explores how different traditions, cultures and schools answer the perennial questions of life and humanity's role within it. Simultaneously, this has provided her with the experiential opportunity to probe far-reaching facets and potentials of human experience. This autoethnographic approach has, and continues to take Helen's research pursuits to new levels. She has a particular interest in the role and potential of medicinal plants in the evolution of consciousness. Her experiences and findings are being compiled in a series of books yet to be titled.

Helen offers one-to-one consultations incorporating energetic techniques of transformation. She also facilitates international tours, guiding and supporting individuals and groups during their journeys of self-exploration and evolution. For more information see www.drhelenkogan.com

Contents

Abbreviations

EA	Emerging Awareness
FoffTing	Finishing-off Thinking
FRT	Frequent Repetitive Thinking
NFR	Natural Frame of Reference
PiCs	People in Charge
T-Topping	Thought-trying-out-process
UC	Ultimate Communion
VTA	Visible Thought Analysis

List of Illustrations

Preface

In 2009, Routledge published *The Science of Acting* which details the theory behind an acting technique developed by Sam Kogan (1946–2004). Kogan taught at numerous London drama schools before founding his own; *The School of The Science of Acting* (now *The Kogan Academy of Dramatic Arts*). Kogan's professional training was at the Russian Academy of Theatre Arts (GITIS) where Konstantin Stanislavsky's pioneering work taught actors to think the thoughts of the characters they were playing.

Early in his teaching career, Kogan recognised that how people think and the creation of believable characters are two fields of study critically linked by the subject of human consciousness. An actor's fundamental tool is his or her thinking and what fundamentally makes people who they are, is their thinking. In exploring the former, Kogan was uncovering a new approach to understanding the latter; he soon found that he was developing more than a scientific framework for performers, he was simultaneously classifying and detailing the workings of the mind in a way that had never been done before.

Throughout Kogan's years of directing and teaching, he repeatedly brought to light the parallels between acting and how people think in their everyday lives. Whether you came for an hour's introductory seminar or a three-year Acting/Directing course, you never left your first day at the Academy with the same thoughts about yourself and life with which you walked in.

The Science of Acting developed over a 35-year period through Kogan's conversations with students and actors. Given the number of people he taught and directed during this time, add to this the number of characters they were each analysing and contemplating, this was a large pool of Consciousnesses or 'sample number' to be working with. That this work and its claims have been thoroughly and repeatedly tested should be a key consideration for the reader.

It should also be noted that as *The Science of Acting* evolved, any final analysis of an individual's thinking (which contributed to general conclusions made about the way we all think), was a result of lengthy discussions and exercises. This process was a steady unveiling by both student and tutor of the *truth* (as will thoroughly be covered in this book) behind an individual's thoughts. By unravelling and identifying the components of an individual's thinking in this way, each person would see their thinking patterns and the 'inputs' that contributed to their thoughts. *The Science of Acting* developed in this way; over many years, through a multitude of people discussing, considering, recognising and identifying the origin and nature of their thinking and the influence this was having on their lives.

The publication of *The Science of Acting* was a memorial to its founder and a milestone for the Academy, making it one of the few drama colleges in the world to document and publish their technique (if they have one, as not all do). As was always to be the case for such a publication, the audience for the book was niched towards actors and directors. It was and continues to be noted, by the many individuals who have read *The Science of Acting* or have crossed paths with this body of knowledge, that its reach is far beyond the realm of the rehearsal room.

Many non-actors purchased *The Science of Acting* and reported it a life-changing read, despite it targeting performers. The demands came early – "When will you write a book for the everyday person and 'take out the acting stuff'?". The non-actors didn't want to keep glazing over the bits they didn't find relevant, even if subsequently admitting the book to be "surprisingly very useful" in many aspects of their everyday lives. The demands became so frequent that the background noise of needing to write *Why We Think the Way We Do and How to Change It* was near-deafening – it was time to take to the computer keyboards. Thomas Garvey, Senior Tutor and Head of Directing at the Academy, and Helen Kogan (Sam's daughter) who compiled and edited *The Science of Acting*, shared the task of bringing *Why We Think the Way We Do and How to Change It* to the page.

The purpose of this book is to create an easy-to-read, self-help tool. Our aim is to provide you with enough information, in sufficient detail, so that what you read makes sense, you can see it work, and crucially – that it makes a difference to your life.

To accurately convey how and what different people think, only real life examples have been included (though names and some personal details have been changed) – and there are many of them at that! The examples are also to show you how universal many of our thoughts are. Certainly we are all different – but not necessarily as different as you may think (if that's what you happen to think).

It is necessary to explain how this work originated for one more reason. It is for you to understand that it has grown out of the curriculum of a three-year acting course, which as you would expect, is a very practical one. Discussions and exercises have always been integral to learning *The Science of Acting* for an experiential understanding of the theory. Exercises, for instance, carried out in front of a tutor or group allow the student to receive feedback and guidance. The benefit being that the tutor can precisely phrase their feedback/comments for the student to easily understand. This aspect of teaching is very hard to convey in written form, however much we bend the rules of writing! Nevertheless, where possible exercises and alternative approaches to exploring the topics have been included, to give you a deeper experience and understanding of what you're reading. There will be things for you to do – and lots to think about!

What we also have to adjust for in converting a classroom into a book is that a live tutor is able to give examples as and when necessary, without seeming pedantic. When writing a book, you don't know how much/little is necessary for each reader. On this we have tried our best to include enough information without labouring the point, however there may be places when you feel you have 'got it' but we're still talking about it. In such cases, try to bear in mind there will be other readers who aren't as quick on that point, and that there may be times when you need more information yourself. It may also be possible that you just *think* you've got it – and any over simplification/emphasis is to ensure otherwise.

From the start, you will find thoughts, memories, ideas and questions coming to mind, so it's a good idea to keep a notebook to hand as you read through the book. The reflections you have will be useful to look back on. It will also benefit you to read this book a few times. It's not that you have to read the book again and again to 'drum it in', rather that each time you read it you will find something new, or more accurately put: it will help you find something new within you! New perspectives and insights of self-understanding will surface each and every time you choose to dip back in.

All major terms are clearly defined within each chapter as well as in the Glossary.

Any other capitalised words are considered minor terms and will briefly be defined in the text (so as not to detract from the main emphasis of the chapter), with their complete definitions in the Glossary.

Some of the terms that are frequently used and critical to this work are lengthy so they have been abbreviated for ease of reading. A list of the abbreviations has been included at the start of this book in case you need to refer back at any stage.

Aside from reading and considering the contents of this book and working on the exercises, it is highly recommended that you work with others in some way. Even simply having a conversation with someone you know and trust, with whom you can share your reflections, will benefit you. Ideally this would be with someone else who is reading *Why We Think the Way We Do and How to Change It*. In this, you will have the advantage of another person's perspective, be asked potentially valuable questions and find answers you might not have otherwise considered.

Then, if you find you would like to take your study of this work even further, workshops and courses are regularly organised and available through the website www.whywethinkthewaywedo.com. As you will soon realise, there is a lot of our thinking that we can't (or don't want to) see for ourselves, which is why observations and comments from another Consciousness, especially those of an experienced tutor, can be invaluable.

Right, now to find out *Why We Think the Way We Do and How To Change It*...

Introduction
The Mind Erosion

There are libraries of books helping humans to understand themselves better, all of which provide useful insights into various aspects of human behaviour. Given this abundance of knowledge, and given that humanity has been around for as long as it has – with everyone doing a lot of thinking in all that time – one wonders why we remain so far from understanding ourselves, given that our problems are so prevalent.

This isn't to say that books haven't improved people's lives and certainly we all have been inspired in various ways by what we have read, but when it comes to self-understanding, despite the knowledge available, people don't seem to change that much. Although we might like to imagine we're changing, the changes are often only superficial and many of our problems are still there, year after year.

Many of us get inspired by a new title, buy the book, take the new information on board, integrate it with what we know, alter a few things in our lives…for a while…and then, not too far down the road, we find that we are back to being faced with the same old problems.

"Why does this happen?", you ask, "And given that I have just paid for this one, will this book be any better? What does this book contain that is going to make a difference?"

Perhaps, for you, relationships are a problem. Relationships that start out enchantingly always end antagonistically? How were those two extremes possible? And why does it keep happening? Why is it that the relationship you wanted to succeed and did everything you could to make succeed, didn't? If you were half of that relationship, why couldn't you see what was coming?

Or is it that your finances are constantly at a critical low, so much so that your stomach tightens whenever you enquire about your bank balance? And no matter how much you earn, money always manages to slip through your fingers?

Do you have a pattern of making friends only for them to reject or abandon you further down the line? Or are you always looking to improve your career but always seem to mess up? Maybe it seems like the whole world is against you? Time and time again circumstances seem to conspire against you.

Why, quite simply, is your life as you want it so perpetually out of reach and however friendly, smart, educated, easy-going, practical, hardworking, enthusiastic or successful you are, there is always something stopping your life from being as you want it? And you probably aren't even asking for much, right?

And even when you can identify the problem, why is it that you are not able to make the changes necessary for your life to be better and stick to it?

Why is it that no matter what books you read, what courses you take and what advice you listen to, you cannot seem to make long lasting changes?

"WHY?!" you yell.

The answer to all of this is fundamentally two things…

and the first is…

you have a Mind Erosion!

What follows is a metaphor to explain what a Mind Erosion is and this will give you an idea of how thoughts, formed within the mind, also form long-lasting limitations on our ability to think freely and live the life we want. The metaphor can be applied to any of the types of thoughts that are discussed throughout this book, so keep this in mind as you continue through the chapters.

Imagine that a man is walking towards you across a field (see Figure A). Imagine that he walks this same route frequently. If he walks across the field three or four times a month, he will leave no impression on the field at all. However, if he walks across the field more often, a path eventually will begin to form. This is called a type of 'land erosion'. In time, the groove that the path has formed makes this path easier to walk than any other part of the field. Naturally, our guy here gets used to this path and begins to feel comfortable choosing it as the only way – and even his preferred way – for getting across the field. Why would he walk any other way?

Figure A. Man walking across a field

Imagine that the field is *your* Consciousness and the path is a thought…let's say a thought about life, that it is lonely. Given that, now imagine getting up out of bed in the morning regretting that no one is there with you. You have breakfast and again, the same thought comes in, regret that no one is there to share it with you. You get to work, and belong with other people, but you feel they don't really care whether you are part of their lives or not, and when you return home there is no one there to greet you. And in this way your life continues.

Each thought you've had since getting out of bed has a degree of 'Life is lonely'. If you think this once or twice a day then it probably won't have a lasting effect but if you think this thought more often, then it becomes a problem. It's a problem because each day these thoughts are thought they are gently but consistently 'digging' a Mind Erosion of the thought 'Life is lonely'. And the more you use this thought the easier it becomes to walk that path, and as you get used to thinking, 'Life is lonely', it begins to feel normal and eventually even comfortable (see Figure B).

Figure B. Man walking along a path

As you repeatedly walk a country path, it becomes a ditch. It's the same with a thought, but in a Mind Erosion the ditch gets deeper and deeper, so that eventually it gets hard to climb, or even see out of (see Figure C). This is how it becomes near-impossible to think any other thought in a given situation (and this is why people will often insist that their 'Life is lonely' or '…unfair' or '…hard', no matter how much evidence or encouragement they are given to see things otherwise. It's as though they have no other path available).

At an earlier stage, when your head was more clearly above ground level, before you were literally 'in so deep', you could still see the rest of the field and the other thoughts that were available for you to think (Figures A and B). Back then, it was easier to step out of the ditch and choose another path. You will have noticed how a young child will very quickly go from crying and wanting care, to smiling and exploring, when a new stimulus is offered. We have all smiled at the few seconds just after a toddler has fallen over, when the child is choosing whether to cry or laugh depending on how onlookers will react. This is the moment when then child is choosing between different thought paths. However, the deeper the ditch, the harder it becomes to change in this way.

Figure C. Man walking inside a ditch

Now compare the toddler above, with a sulky teenager who won't budge on a decision no matter the options offered. The deeper the ditches are trodden, the more normal it feels to walk them...and in time you don't even recognise that you are in a ditch (Figure C). This is why, when you are given the opportunity to climb out of a ditch and take another 'path', you (often greatly) resist it.

What we want to emphasise here is that although you might think you want to change the way you live, having a Mind Erosion means in some sense you *don't*. You are in fact so comfortable with living/thinking the way you do, that to change would make you feel insecure and put you out of what you may consider your 'comfort zone'. But don't worry, because once you understand that this is the reason you feel insecure, you will – by using this book – be able to make lasting changes in your life.

Mind Erosion
Paths or patterns of thinking followed
irrespective of visible circumstances

Understanding Mind Erosions is fundamental to understanding *Why We Think The Way We Do* and to being able to *Change It*. In every chapter from here on you will learn about the different contributory factors that created your Mind Erosion. You may be surprised how embedded certain ways of thinking have become, how deep in your ditch you have found yourself and how automatic (rigid Mind Erosion) this thinking is. Essentially, you will learn why and how your Mind Erosion has formed the way it has and you will be provided with the tools to deconstruct it – so that you can live with greater freedom – thinking the thoughts you want to think, rather than the thoughts you have automatically and rigidly been thinking for years.

Now, going back, we stated that there are *two* fundamental reasons for not being able to change the way you think. The second reason can be approached with a question about the first:

Why is that I haven't noticed my Mind Erosion before?

One thing is clear – whatever is in the way of you improving your life, you can't see it. Otherwise you sure as hell would have done something about it, right? You haven't seen what the problem is to be able to fix it, so in not *seeing* 'it', 'it' must be invisible – so to speak.

This means your Mind Erosions are invisible to you!

"Oh for crying out loud!", you say, "What chance does that give me?"

Well, don't despair. Just because you haven't seen your Mind Erosions before doesn't mean you can't see them, otherwise this book would be pointless.

Subconscious

'Subconscious' or 'unconscious' (the term preferred in psychoanalysis) are words that imply a dark murky region of thoughts where one is lost if one enters. We use these words in everyday language to describe an area of our minds where we suspect some of our thoughts might be – but don't know for sure. The subconscious/unconscious implies an area that is unknowable, somewhere where the thoughts are all a 'stab in the dark'. It's considered a location that we can guess at but we might as well forget about as we have no chance of clearly seeing anything there: "Oh yeah, I guess subconsciously I might think that but..."

But this is not true. The very premise of this book is precisely that one's subconscious is something that *can* be seen; its elements can be identified, mapped out, and confusions can be ordered and understood. For us to move ahead in this vein, we will rarely use the word subconscious and will instead refer to thoughts you haven't seen as 'unaware'. This is because 'unaware' doesn't have the same vague connotations as 'subconscious'.

Also note, we will use the words 'visible' and 'invisible' interchangeably with the words 'aware' and 'unaware' respectively, for convenience and clarity. In short, thoughts are either seen (you are **aware** of them or equally, they are **visible** to you) or are not seen (you are **unaware** of them or they are **invisible** to you).

With that clarified let us proceed to see what we can see.

***

We are at the start of an enthralling journey of self-discovery, where the term 'self-development' will barely do the subject justice.

As was said, what happens when we read an inspirational book is that for a while we are genuinely motivated to change our lives. But(!) our Mind Erosion has become so deep and rigid over the years that *it* wants to think itself, no matter how illogical, dysfunctional or contrary to our conscious thinking, which genuinely wants to change. It's our rigid Mind Erosion that consistently pulls us back to the same old patterns of thinking… "Ahh yes, back to this comfy path to stroll down, the one I had before all the disruption – it's good to be back".

And there you are.

Back to where you were.

To change deep patterns of thinking and behaviour we need to see the thoughts that have hereto been invisible to us and understand our Mind Erosion.

Crucially, we want to expose the ditches that don't want us to 'get ahead', 'develop', 'have a life' and 'be free'.

This book is written to provide you with the tools to do so.

PART 1
WHY WE THINK
THE WAY WE DO

Chapter One
Awareness

Brian is 11 years-old and standing at the front of the queue to jump over the gymnastics horse in gym class. Sitting on the horse is Tracy, a classmate who is holding up the proceedings by striking various glamorous poses. After a few moments of watching this, Brian marches up to Tracy and pushes her off the horse consequently breaking her arm. When asked why he did this, Brian could genuinely not come up with an answer, he was completely blank.

Why couldn't Brian find an answer? He had pushed Tracy deliberately and must have had a reason but no answer surfaced, not even when asked 25 years later.

What Brian lacked was an Awareness of his own thinking.

But what does Awareness mean?

Awareness can be defined as 'being in the-here-and-now' or 'being in the moment' or 'conscious knowledge'... but these terms are a little too vague to be helpful.

Many more definitions for Awareness exist, where some are more precise than others, but if we are looking for reasons as to *Why We Think The Way We Do*, then for our definition to be most useful, it needs to take into account the thoughts which govern our lives.

In Brian's case, understanding what Awareness means would be to explain the thoughts which made him do what he did. Like Brian, we've all had times when we have done things and not known why we did them, this indicates that we were thinking things and not knowing what we were thinking.

Taking this a step further, this means that to be aware, we need to be able to see our thinking.

Very simply, we can then say that Awareness is the ability to see one's own thinking.

Given this clear definition, when talking about Awareness there are two (perhaps obvious) parameters that we need to consider; that being the thinking which we *can see* (that which we are aware of) and the thinking which we *cannot see* (that which we are unaware of). It was this latter kind of thinking, the unaware kind, that made Brian (an example of all of us) do what he did, and not understand why he did it.

To repeat, as we will be referring to these terms throughout the book, thoughts we can see and are aware of are called *aware* or *visible* thoughts and thoughts we can't see and aren't aware of are called *unaware* or *invisible* thoughts.

Aware thoughts are thoughts we all have like 'Bus', 'Pretty girl', 'Nice coffee', 'That guy's an asshole', 'I'd better hurry' or simple images of things or places like 'Book', 'Carpet' or 'Helsinki'. Aware thoughts exist to help us orient our way through each day.

Now, building on our definition of Awareness as the ability to see one's own thinking; to *increase* our Awareness we need to start looking for the thoughts we haven't been able to see – the unaware thoughts.

Does this mean we are looking to make all our thinking visible?

No, not at all.

Not only would it be impossible to see *all* the thinking we have *all* the time but it would also be unbearable. This could be why nature designed our Consciousness to allow us to see only a very small part of it at any time.

We have a *lot* of thoughts you see!!

And if you haven't realised this by now, you soon will.

Aside from having visible orientating thoughts – like 'Bus', 'Pretty girl', etc. – we also have *intentions;* what we visibly decide we are going to do. These aren't as straightforward as orientating thoughts. Decisions about how we are going to live do not tend to be processed visibly. A simple example to consider is making the decision to change your pattern of always being late. One day you decide, 'From now on I am going to be on time' – only, when the next day arrives, you find yourself late for a meeting again and you can't understand why. So much for visible intentions and the thoughts we can see!

A priority of this book is to help you see your invisible thoughts because of their fundamental role in *Why You Think the Way You Do.* As a reminder, invisible thoughts are all the thoughts our Consciousness has decided we do not need (or do not *want*) to be visible. They can be anything from a random memory of being a child and eating an ice cream one day, to very influential thoughts about life, ourselves and other people.

Returning to the example of deciding to be on time and yet still being late and not understanding why; this logically points to us having invisible wants. Invisible wants which override visible intentions.

"But hang on…!", you shout, "…there are times when I decide to do something and I then do it".

This is true; these are times when your invisible wants match your visible ones and this is when you feel you are 'getting ahead' and 'making progress' in your life.

The problem (now take this next bit slowly) lies in your invisible wants not matching your visible wants and especially when they contradict each other. This is when frustration or confusion builds up, when you think you want something or your life to go a certain way, but it doesn't happen, or doesn't go as you planned (e.g. wanting to be on time but something stops you from doing so). It's like driving with the gas and the breaks on at the same time – you can't!

Perhaps re-read the last paragraph for it to fully sink in.

Later we will explore contradicting thoughts but for now, let's have a closer look at how we can know that invisible thoughts exist if we can't see them.

Have you ever noticed that when you're on your own you have mood swings that have no explanation? You don't know what caused your mood to change as there was no outside influence, all you know is that one minute you're happy and the next you're sad.

Do you often make agreements with yourself which you easily break? Having a lot to prepare for the following day you get home from work and decide that you aren't going to watch the television… and yet half an hour later you find yourself on the sofa, remote control in hand.

Do you repeatedly do things that you regret like eating chocolate, arriving late for work or smoking?

Do you have thoughts about, or relationships with people that you don't want to have: "Why can't I stop arguing with Mary?"? and you can only find feeble reasons for doing so.

Have you ever had times when you did or said something and thought, "I have no idea why I did that…what was I thinking?"?

Here's a particularly interesting one – do you remember seeing your parents do things which you thought were not right, embarrassing or even disgusting, and you promised yourself you would never do those things and yet now and again, you catch yourself doing those exact things?

What's common to all these examples?

Again, it's that there is thinking in our heads which we cannot see but which overrides our visible wants, and subsequently runs large parts of our lives!

Have you ever said something like, "I didn't want to but I couldn't stop myself"?

Isn't it interesting, perhaps even profound to recognise that there exist situations when *I* couldn't stop *myself*.

Or, "*I* couldn't help *myself*, I had to do it".

There are other phrases like this…you may know or use them:
"I wasn't paying attention to what I was doing."
"I let myself down."
"I've been giving myself a hard time over this all day."

Do you see that we have an unacknowledged recognition of a second 'I' within us, an 'I' which doesn't always follow the first 'I's plan?

We have an understanding that invisible thinking exists but we are either unable or unwilling to look at it.

So how do visible and invisible thinking work within our Consciousness?

Here's a simple example to start with, it's to show you that there are thoughts that are not in your head at this moment but are still in your mind somewhere:

Take a moment to think about your kitchen.

…

…

What happened?

It became a visible thought. You saw a picture of it in your mind. But where was it before? Where was 'Kitchen' before you read the word above? Wherever it was you couldn't see it. It was invisible. When you read the word it easily went from being invisible to being visible.

Awareness and Visible Thinking

Imagine a pond or pool of water which, when you look down into it from above, you see the top 20 cm (arbitrary distance) below the surface. You see the fish that swim into this area and you can see other plant life that exists there. Beyond 20 cm depth, however, it becomes difficult to see and at some distance a little further down you can't see a thing (Figure 1.1).

Figure 1.1 Pool of Awareness

Imagine your mind is this pool of water and the two layers of visible (upper 20 cm) and invisible (beneath 20 cm) thinking are separated by an indistinct line. The surface layer we call the 'Layer of Visible Thinking' and, as its name suggests, this is the area where visible thoughts can be seen – many call this the 'Mind's Eye'. Below the Layer of Visible Thinking are the thoughts that you cannot see, and this is where your invisible thoughts reside.

When you were asked to read the word 'kitchen', the thought became visible, as though the Layer of Visible Thinking dropped deeper. The thought 'Kitchen' is something that is part of your everyday life: You are in your kitchen a few times a day or you think about 'Kitchen' when you think about what you're going to prepare there when you get home. It's easy to lower the Layer of Visible Thinking for 'Kitchen' to be seen because thinking 'Kitchen' is a frequent occurrence for you.

OK, continuing, now think about the following:

What you had for lunch last Thursday.

...

...

The last birthday party you went to.

...

...

How you felt on your first day of school.

...

...

These are probably a little tougher than thinking about your kitchen, right?

These are thoughts that are normally invisible to you but with time or with a memory prompt, you are able to see them.

Another way to imagine Awareness is that it's like bringing a powerful torch to the pool, one that can illuminate down to a deeper level. The longer the torch shines, the more of the pool can be seen, lighting up thoughts and memories from the (previously invisible) depths of the pool. As you begin to see some of the thoughts that were once invisible and have now been illuminated, the haze from immediately below 20 cm clears, giving you a larger viewing depth. You are now seeing more of your invisible thoughts because you have increased the size of your Layer of Visible Thinking. By increasing the size of your Layer of Visible Thinking, you are increasing your Awareness...

Which is the very Purpose of this book and especially Part One.

Awareness
The ability to see one's own thinking

Note: The aim of increasing or expanding one's Awareness is not for the Layer of Visible Thinking to take up the whole pool and for it to be completely clear but for this layer to enlarge as and when you need it to. Also, note that the Layer of Visible Thinking doesn't need to remain at any particular depth. What *is* important, however, is for you to know that you can increase its size any time you want to see what you really think…or when you want to look for invisible thoughts.

Why is Awareness and seeing our invisible thinking so important?

As you get further into this book you will see that most of what you do, say and think is dictated by your invisible thoughts. Once you see these thoughts and how they affect your life, you will be able to choose the thoughts you want to keep (the ones that benefit your life), and notice the ones that are hindrances – we will come to what you can do about these in Part Two. Without understanding how your Awareness works, much of your pool is dark and you have no way of knowing what you think, let alone be able to change it – and your life – in a positive way.

We need visible and invisible thoughts because as discussed, the brain needs a filter on what we can see; keeping that which is useful for our daily functioning and holding back that which gets in the way. What we must consider with this filter is that while it exists to assist us in our everyday lives, if there are thoughts that we would prefer (for whatever reason) not to see, they will stay hidden from us within the invisible, murky portion of the pool. The reason for this is that usually the first time we experienced these thoughts they generated so much fear, shame or suffering that we didn't want to see them again, so our Consciousness allowed these thoughts to become invisible. These invisible unwanted thoughts have remained invisible but as we will continue to find out, they powerfully run our lives.

Fortunately, for those who want to change, this is a reversible process and this book is preparing you to look at what you haven't been able to see before. The Finishing-off Thinking chapter in Part Two is dedicated to helping you look at the thoughts that have caused you suffering, frustration and failure in your life, and help you understand that everybody has these kinds of thoughts. You will be able to see the thoughts for what they are – just thoughts (yes, that's all!) – and you will learn how to finish them off, so they no longer play a governing role in your Consciousness.

No – don't jump to that chapter now!

The order of the chapters of this book has been thought through, each building on the one before. Everything that you read between now and then are the steps that you need to take on the way there.

Emerging Awareness

The bedrock of psychotherapy is the influence of early-life events on our thoughts and behaviour as adults, this being for good reason. From the moment we are born through to around our teenage years, randomly yet periodically, we have experiences that are captured in our heads as what seem like ethereal photographs or short films. Yes, we are talking about memories. In particular we are interested in the memories that imprint themselves on our minds, and as we are about to delve into, the ones that have specific impact on our thinking in later life. These are what we call our Emerging Awareness (EA).

Emerging Awareness
The first perceived and most remembered episodes from one's life

Understanding the influence of EA on our Awareness, and inextricably on our lives, is a critical subject and worthy of putting under the magnifying glass. Which is what we are about to do.

People remember varying amounts from their early lives. For example, looking back at your life, your first memory could be of your parents on your second birthday; then perhaps one of staring at swirls in a carpet pattern sometime later, then your next memory comes a year after that; of playing with a worm in the garden with the sun on your back, then a few months or a year after that another experience gets stuck as a memory.

What is interesting is that although many of these early memories seem very insignificant, they are some of the most important influences on our lives. Otherwise why remember them at all?

What follows is a memory belonging to a man called James. This is the memory as he recalled it, before he 'thought it through':

James, aged four or five, is travelling with his parents and several older siblings. They are on a train returning from a seaside town in England, back to London where they live. His parents buy Second Class tickets (as they were then called) and join a very packed train. Unable to find seats in Second Class, they see an empty First Class compartment and decided to sit there where they end up filling the compartment. Part way through the journey, James' sister goes to the toilet leaving a seat free, soon after which a man comes along the corridor obviously looking for a seat. As the man starts to slide the door to the compartment open, James jumps up and tells the man that the empty seat is his sister's and so the man leaves.

This was the memory as James had always remembered it. He never thought much about it; as to whether there was any more to it or if there were any other thoughts attached. However, when asked to think around the memory, other bits of information started to appear and an impression emerged pointing to a deeper meaning to this memory.

James remembered that after the man who was looking for the seat left, all the members of his family laughed out loud because, at four or five years old James was the youngest of the family. In discussion with adult James, the question arose as to why he, the youngest of them all, jumped up to dismiss the man. The answer hit him square in the face – because (he thought) he was the only one who could.

This sounds like a strange answer coming from the youngest in the family. James' reasoning was that he thought all the other family members were afraid of being discovered for having the wrong tickets. Adult James paused and reflected upon this…he realised that something didn't fully add up. He still hadn't reached the core of it; of understanding the thoughts that he had, which lead to his actions. With a little more reflection, James saw that his family members' fear was only partly to do with having cheaper tickets than they should have for the carriage they were in. Adult James was now able to identify a greater fear that lay underneath, which was that all his family members shared thoughts of inferiority. That was it! James had instinctively known their discomfort and that the situation with the tickets had exacerbated this, and *this* was why he had jumped to the rescue!

A sense of inferiority usually originates in childhood and we should note that, to James, it was apparent that the sense of inferiority had passed from his parents to his siblings and so he was protecting them all. James, uniquely, did not share this feeling of being less than others because at the time he wasn't old enough to have adopted this thinking. This was exactly why he felt that only *he* could protect his family.

At the time, young James didn't think through all the above, he simply acted in the moment. It was only as an adult looking back that these answers surfaced and matched the impression he had of why he did what he did. The tickets, or any official outcome of being in the wrong compartment didn't matter to James, all he wanted to do was protect his family from humiliation. Here you should know that James' parents were immigrants with strong foreign accents and James felt that if they spoke, then they would 'give themselves away'. Being an immigrant obviously doesn't make you inferior but James felt that his parents thought their backgrounds made them inferior in Britain. James jumped to his family's 'rescue' before anyone else could, because he thought that only *he* could protect the family from the humiliation of being found out, and the likelihood of being asked to leave their seats.

Did you notice in the last line of an earlier paragraph that 'he thought' appeared, like this – (he thought) – in brackets. This is to emphasise that it doesn't matter what we might think he should have thought or what we think we would have thought – what is important is what *he* thought because it is *his* thoughts that influence his life. An individual's logic is not necessarily objective.

How did this memory and the associated thinking affect James' adult life?

The conclusion James made from his memory was that he had wanted to protect his family; they are people he cares about and who he wants to belong with. Now, as he grows up, if he wants to continue to belong with his family what does he need to do? How do we belong with a group of people or someone we feel is important to us in some way? Usually by being like them, by espousing the same or similar beliefs or opinions and (more invisibly) adopting the same or similar relationship they have with their life.

In this case, James knew that to belong with his family he would have to adopt their same feeling of inferiority (just like his siblings had done before him), and as he grew up that's exactly what he did.

It's important to note that whether it is a feeling of inferiority or superiority, of being rejected or doing the rejecting (or both states, depending on the situation), all humans overridingly want to belong, and so we adopt many of our parents' thoughts to do so…despite the outcome.

Back to James…

As he grew up he increasingly 'became' inferior to belong with his family *and* he (unawarely) developed a strategy to protect himself from the humiliation that was the result of thinking of himself as inferior. As an adult, James always finds ways to avoid exposure to uncertain situations in the way that he thought his parents were exposed to on that train journey. When James is not completely sure of the set-up of an event like social engagements, restaurants, parties, clubs, meetings etc. he will either worry about it and/or seek reassurance that the circumstances are familiar before considering attending. Or he will simply not go. This is because James believes any of these situations could lead to him standing out as inferior to others – which would be excruciatingly uncomfortable for him.

It doesn't matter that James' family are not with him or even that the train incident happened so long ago. This is because the EA acts (as it does for everyone) in what we call a 'Life Situation'.

Life Situation
A set of circumstances that set a precedent for future events and behaviours, regardless of the context and relevancy

This means that although what happened to James as a child was a unique incident, James' interpretation of what took place went on to influence all aspects of his future life. James described this particular Life Situation as being a "Third Class citizen with Second Class tickets in a First Class environment". In the long term, James would go on to continually see life as a series of regrets and missed opportunities because of all the occasions he avoided, to prevent the slightest possibility of humiliation.

Of course it's possible to develop harmless or positive thoughts from an EA, however, in most cases we tend to (and this is why we are discussing it) develop highly influential, dysfunctional thoughts from them, leading to the formation of generalised thoughts. Generalised thoughts are our conclusions about aspects of life as well as life itself. These thoughts form a template that we use to interpret future experiences – we will go into this in detail in Chapter Six (Mindprint). For now, you only need to know that the three most common generalised thoughts we have are about ourselves, about life and about people.

Using James' EA on the train as an example, you can see how he could have concluded the following generalised thoughts:
'I am burdened' (with an unwanted responsibility)
'Life is uncertain' (not knowing when the next potential humiliation will come)
'People are free' (to enjoy life without stress)

James' EA involved a specific event but as mentioned at the start of this chapter, we also have many memories that seem to be a snap-shot of a seemingly unimportant moment in time, as though we've captured it by accident or randomly. This is because an EA usually happens as a summary of unaware thoughts an individual is having about their lives at the time.

For instance, if you have an EA with guilt at its core, it's likely that guilt was a general part of your life at that time (interestingly, it is often the case that impressions like guilt can play such a general part in someone's life that they wouldn't even know it was there, it had become so normal). So, seemingly unimportant memories like staring at swirls on a carpet can have greater significance behind them. For instance, a child may be losing themselves while looking at the carpet swirls because their parents are rowing in another room; a situation that happened a lot at the time. The individual may grow up simply remembering time spent staring at the swirls, but unawarely there will be a lot of (often, unpleasant) thoughts attached to that simple memory.

James' memory is a typical EA as a first or early memory but EAs can also be from later in childhood when a particular memory has clung to our Consciousness. Look out for when you say things like, "I don't know why but I always seem to remember this time when…" or "This memory has always stuck in my head when…" or "It's funny that I always think of…" Or words to this effect.

The impact of an EA on who we become cannot be underestimated and this is why looking at your memories and how they affect your life today is so useful in helping you increase your Awareness. The key to increasing your Awareness is to ask questions. That is why there are so many in this book; they help you see further into the pool.

Although it may seem like we question our lives all the time, like "Why did that happen?" or "Why does Mary make me react in that way?" in truth, most people only ask themselves very superficial questions. This often leads to only very superficial responses: "It just did", "That's just Mary being Mary", "That's just who I am". Or, if an answer doesn't come immediately, we lose ourselves in other thoughts, like: "If I can't get the answer now I'll never get it…I may as well just…".

And the water in the pool stays as unclear as it was.

But… with a little more effort, deeper answers will start to come.

In this book it is assumed you want answers to questions you may have never known to ask or didn't know how to answer.

To increase your Awareness, you have to ask questions about the circumstances of your earliest memories; about how you felt at the time, what thoughts were there, what impressions you have now, and whether/how these things are connected.

Who was there?
How old was I?
How was I dressed?
Do these facts add up?
Are the circumstances logical?
What was I doing before?
What did I do after?
Do I have an impression of that time, one that I can't make sense of?
Can I now find words to try and define this impression?

And don't give up when the answers do not immediately come!

Also notice other EAs surfacing, their circumstances may be different but they likely share the same thoughts at their core. This, in turn, can lead you down other paths of self-exploration, shining a light on other areas of your thinking that you could not previously see.

Looking at EAs is an important and engrossing process in which you will increasingly see more of your thinking and how your experiences have shaped your life. With each new discovery, you will find numerous answers to puzzles that have probably nagged at you for years. The more aware you become of the patterns of thinking running your life, the more you are weakening the ones you no longer want to have.

To end this chapter, here are some examples of EAs from people's lives and the generalised thoughts which accompanied them:

Mariana is four years old and her mother has taken her to see a bullfight. During the interval, a donkey is brought on for a child to feed a carrot to. Unbeknownst to Mariana she has been chosen and so her mother starts carrying her towards the bullring to feed the donkey. Mariana, who thinks she is being taken to the ring to encounter the bull, starts kicking and screaming as her mother tries to hand her over to the bullfighter. Mariana is in such an uncontrollable state that her mother has to take her back to her seat. Back at her seat, Mariana discovers that another girl is now being taken into the bullring to feed the donkey. Not only is Mariana upset that her mother hadn't explained to her in the first place why she was being taken down to the bullring, she also regrets that another girl has taken her place in what would have been an enjoyable experience.

The generalised thoughts that Mariana took from this experience were: Life is a disappointment, Life is unfair, People make me fail – if my mother had explained it, I would have had a nice experience, now I have nothing but regrets.

Pétur is about two years old and is standing on a chair in the kitchen. His mother is with him. His dad isn't at home and is away working. Pétur doesn't think his mother is happy and he wants to belong with her. He asks her if he can have some sparkling water and she says "You won't like it" and then gives him some. Upon drinking it, Pétur thinks 'It doesn't taste nice but it's bearable', and he pulls a face. Seeing her son's expression change Pétur's mother says "I told you, you wouldn't like it," with some enjoyment.

The generalised thoughts that Pétur took from this experience were: I know I can't solve her loneliness but I will do whatever it takes to make her feel better for a bit – I am a sex-slave or sex-toy.

Mark is six years old and in the back garden with his dad who is trying to fix Mark's bicycle. Mark can see his dad wants to help him but he can also see that his dad doesn't really know what needs to be done. Mark knows what to do to fix his bike but he doesn't want to tell his dad how to do it as this might humiliate him. Mark keeps quiet in the hope his dad will eventually work it out and then he can have his bike back and belong with his dad. His dad never works it out.

The generalised thoughts that Mark took from this experience were: I must not show my true potential, People are a burden (because I must suffer less-capable people (bosses, co-workers, friends etc.), I want to fail so as to belong.

Lesley is about three years old and is travelling in the car with her five year old sister and their mother. Her mother has just left her father and is driving up the motorway crying. The engine catches fire and her mother is in a state of extreme stress and panic. Lesley feels her own sense of fear and panic that she isn't being taken care of properly and thinks 'This woman can't take care of me' and 'My survival is at the whim of others'. The generalised thoughts that Lesley took from this experience were: Life is unpredictable, Life is dangerous, I am alone.

EXERCISE 1

Tell a friend all that you remember about a memory and allow them to ask you questions about it.

See where this takes you.

Chapter Two
Complexes

Coke.

What thought went through your mind when you read this word?
A pile of white powder?
Columbian drug barons?

Or a brown fizzy drink?
Did it come with vodka, ice and a slice?
Or hamburger and a side of fries?
The image of a brand name? In a can or in a bottle?

How about 'stick of chalk'?
What comes to mind?
A new stick? Or is it half worn down?
Is it white or coloured?
What other thoughts come up?
Teacher? Blackboard?

Now, 'water'.
A tap?
The ocean?
Rain?
A glass?

Do you see that the word you are given prompts a thought, which triggers other thoughts? These other thoughts are called 'Affinities'. What's interesting is that these Affinities come into your mind without you asking or looking for them. This is because Affinities are activated *automatically*.

In just these few lines we have covered the main elements of a Complex, which is a group of thoughts, where one thought automatically activates others. Another crucial component (you'll see why see later) is that you are not in control of this activation happening, it takes place whether you like it or not.

Let's try another prompt.

'Football'

...

...

What came in then?
Did you see the ball and its design or a football pitch?
Your son playing football? Perhaps your brother? Or a team of professionals?
Did you get an impression of the texture of the ball?
The smell? Its bounce?
Was it dirty or clean?

Could you stop yourself having these thoughts?
No.

Whatever surfaced for you was part of your 'Football' Complex, where football is the main thought, and the Affinities are connected to it.

Like a shoal of fish which follow each other around everywhere, when you call one fish (one, you think, individual thought) in, the whole bunch of other fish swim in too... invited or not.

These simple examples demonstrate how thoughts are stuck to each other. In fact, there is no such thing as a loose, random or drifting thought; all thoughts are attached to other thoughts. Because of this, seemingly random thoughts can be found to be connected.

Neil woke up one morning and orientated to being 'awake', simultaneously another thought popped into his visible thinking, a memory of the 'Eiffel Tower'. Although the two thoughts, 'I'm awake' and 'Eiffel Tower' seem unrelated they *are* connected through a series of Complexes (Figure 2.1).

A. The visible thought 'I'm awake' is part of Neil's Complex of *Morning*
B. The Complex of *Morning*, for Neil, includes 'Coffee' which connects to his Complex of *Breakfast*
C. Neil's Complex of *Breakfast* is comprised of 'Cigarette' which is part of his Complex of *Socialising*
D. Neil regularly socialises in 'Pubs and clubs' which connects his Complex of *Socialising* to his Complex of *Dancing*
E. Dancing, for Neil, includes memories of clubbing in 'Ibiza' as part of his *Holidays* Complex. Another holiday Neil had was in Paris and this brought up the visible thought 'Eiffel Tower'

Figure 2.1 Complexes and Awareness

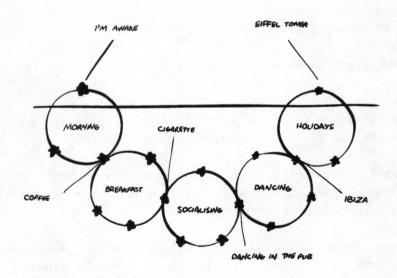

Although this example is mundane (and perhaps seemingly convoluted), it illustrates how several connected thoughts can instantaneously and simultaneously appear in your mind, while appearing to be nonsensical. As you increasingly explore your thinking, there will be times when similar, seemingly unrelated thoughts or memories appear in your visible thinking; ones that have far more serious implications on your life than in Neil's example. Unlocking the links of these, however loosely connected thoughts, is an important part of the process.

Complexes are also part of other Complexes. Imagine one morning you are buying a 'Toasted sandwich' on the way to work. 'Toasted sandwich' is part of your 'Breakfast' Complex. Breakfast is part of your 'Meals' Complex, which is part of your 'Food' Complex, which is part of your 'Health' Complex, which is part of your 'Wellbeing' Complex and so on…

Every Complex is part of a slightly bigger Complex, which is part of another slightly bigger Complex and so on…until we finally arrive at the Super Complex of Complexes! Here, all Complexes are connected and we can call this an individual's Consciousness.

The simple mechanism of Complexes is the foundation on which all our thinking is based. Complexes can be likened to the building blocks of the mind. Notice that some Complexes are simple associations, like 'Pen and Paper' or 'Needle and Thread'. There are, however, others that are more complicated; for instance, 'Eating' is a Complex comprised of the sensation of hunger, the impression of biting, chewing, swallowing and various types of food, their flavours, textures, origins, health implications, preferences, aversions, implications on self-worth…etc.

Some Complexes exist to help us practically navigate through life, like the Complex which reminds us where our house is when we leave work, or where the milk aisle is at the supermarket. These simple Complexes have little effect on our overall thinking. There are however, more intricate Complexes like 'Sex' or 'Money' which are more 'involved' for our Consciousness. Compared to 'Needle and Thread' you can see how more personalised (and involved!) the Complex of 'Sex' is for one person compared to another.

Complex
An interconnected group of thoughts where when one is
activated then so are the others to different degrees

We are going look at how some simple Complexes were originally formed to get a better feel for how they work.

Most of us don't remember when we learned to tie our shoelaces or brush our teeth, but watching children learn behaviours like these for the first time demonstrates the amount of attention required to form a Complex.

The first time a child ties their shoelaces or brushes their teeth, the experiences are completely new. Each individual movement is a new thought, and needs to be practised very slowly for the child to get their fingers (and thoughts!) around it. Each part of the sequence is very easy to forget, not just the movements required at each stage, but also each step in the sequence. The second run-through is often like the first, with the third being only slightly easier. This is then practised over and over until, at some point, the child can do it all without orientating.

This example demonstrates how most Complexes are formed, by Frequent Repetitive Thinking (FRT). We touched on this process in the Introduction when we explained how Mind Erosions come into being – by frequently and repetitively thinking particular thoughts.

Going back to tying the shoelaces...
Here we saw how, as children, we *awarely* formed a Complex. That is, we voluntarily decided to create the Complex, as is the case with all *awarely formed* Complexes, like brushing our teeth, making an omelette and saying something like "Bless you" after someone sneezes. This delineation needs to be made because Complexes are also formed *unawarely*; this happens when Complexes are introduced to our thinking (again, frequently and repetitively over time) in a way that we don't notice happening.

Ivan Pavlov's famous experiments with dogs perfectly illustrates unawarely formed Complexes. In the 1890s, while Pavlov was studying dogs' digestive mechanisms, he rang a bell while feeding a pair of dogs. Then one day,

Pavlov just rang the bell and observed that the dogs start to salivate and look for food. The dogs had formed a Complex because FRT had connected the ringing of the bell with being fed.

The Complex of 'Food and Bell' was repeatedly introduced to the dogs' thinking and then one day their response to the bell became automatic and out of their control. This faculty is also true of humans; a song will trigger very specific memories for us, irrespective of our volition. We don't, at the time, think, 'I must remember this song in relation to this event'; the song was simply part of the Complex of thoughts formed in that moment.

All quite straightforward.

Now, here's the thing:
The formation of Complexes depends, to a very large extent, on how repetitively and frequently you think or do certain things. This means that any(!) things – meaning *anything(!)* – can become a Complex, regardless of how dysfunctional, bizarre, abusive or self-abusive it may be or it becomes.

Oh.

Is that then good or bad for us?

It's not so much a matter of them being either, but it *is* about recognising how these Complexes work, how they affect our everyday thinking, and being able to change whatever isn't working for us or is making us unhappy. You see, a prevalent human tendency is to look outside of ourselves for the cause of our unhappiness and to then blame people and happenings for it: The boss… the girlfriend… the pills… the government… the weather… the neighbour…. However, it is often a Complex in itself to think *these thoughts* (of blame, grudges and resentment) whenever anything unsatisfactory occurs, rather than look to ourselves for the root cause.

Let's leave this here for now. We will return to this theme a few times as the book progresses.

Fundamentally, creating Complexes is the mechanism of learning – you probably 'got' this by now. Without Complexes, we would never have got past the childhood stage of realising that sticking our finger in a flame hurts or that washing powder tastes bad, let alone being able to write a 2000-word essay.

The first Complexes we learned as babies were to do with survival; our mother's smell and that the nipple means food… That's how vital Complexes are to our survival and growth.

Notice that you don't visibly think about most of the Complexes you have learned. This is because Complexes quickly and easily become unaware processes. We don't think about tying our laces despite the mental instructions unawarely playing out as soon as we bend down to do our shoes up. Once Complexes are set, our visible thinking is freed up to think other things.

The process of Complexes becoming unaware is also important for our survival. Evolving humans needed to know that large animals with sharp teeth were dangerous and seeing them meant they should start running in the opposite direction. If they had to consciously reprocess this information every time they would waste valuable seconds. Can you imagine coming face-to-face with a growling lion each week and thinking, "So who's this guy again?…", "What should I do?…" The Complex had to kick in *unawarely*.

Over the years, you will have experienced something like driving a car while thinking about something else (maybe your dinner later that evening, a conversation you had earlier that day…) and then realised that many miles had passed where you weren't awarely thinking about driving. And yet, unawarely, your driving Complex knew what to do.

Unaware thinking is a big part of what makes us human. The physiologist Benjamin Libet recorded electrical brain activity to demonstrate that when humans do simple things like moving their hand, a massive surge (much more than was required to actuate the movement) in brain activity took place *before* the person had consciously decided to do it. This suggests that decision-making involves brain activity that isn't part of our conscious thinking. In Libet's words: "Subconscious activity precedes and determines conscious decisions"[1]. Unaware thinking is part of how we are designed, we have to accept this and also understand what this implies.

To fully grasp how Complexes affect us, you need to understand that we do not live rationally – this has been touched on several times and we will continue to.

No matter how much we would like to think otherwise, we do not walk through life reasoning every situation in its immediacy. Instead, because of Complexes, we are 'wired' to repeat certain patterns of behaviour. So, while it may seem like we are making our own rational and aware choices on a daily basis, these decisions are instead a result of past conditioning playing itself out. As it has been doing for many years.

This isn't a problem if you want to know where to buy milk or when you need to remember a chat-up line...but there is a cautionary side to how Complexes work. A problem for humanity is that, for most of us, the need to survive in the wild is no longer the main objective of everyday life. This need for survival, in a sense, kept us in check – it negated thoughts and behaviours which weren't good for us. Today, most of us know we can survive, we barely think about it. Instead we are constantly preoccupied with being happy. Where this gets complicated, is that happiness means many different things depending on our conditioning. And again, our 'Happiness Complex' can be anything, no matter how dysfunctional!

We have established that our Consciousness informs all our patterns of behaviour by associating thoughts, and once these associations or Complexes have been thought often or intensely enough they then repeat themselves – no matter what we awarely may think about the results. This is another example of our Mind Erosion.

Smoking is an example of a very strong Complex. As we have seen, a Complex is something we learn and when it comes to smoking this is something that is very hard to 'unlearn'. Smoking is a Complex that is formed between the mental picture of a cigarette, the physiological effect it has, the circumstances in which we smoke and (as you will see in a later chapter) the Purpose associated with it. It is difficult for many people to stop smoking because, on top of the addictive chemical ingredients, the thoughts within the Complex have has very strong links. This means that however much you may know about the ill effects, the Complex is so strong that immediately after the last mouthful of a meal or each time you step into a bar the only thing you can think to do is…yes, light up!

The strongest Complexes are formed during childhood and these go on to become important Complexes in adulthood. Let's look at Monique as an example: Monique's parents seem, to her, to be relatively uninterested in her school life and will even discourage her from aspiring to anything. For instance, when Monique talks about something she is looking forward to, her mother's response is usually, "Don't count your chickens before they hatch". Monique understands this to mean, 'Don't get your hopes up as it probably won't happen' (you may interpret this differently but remember, it is important to understand that this is Monique's interpretation of what is being said). The constant flattening of her hopes and aspirations makes Monique feel that her mother doesn't want her to succeed.

Over the longer-term, the responses from Monique's mother take place regularly, not necessarily every day, but over the course of her formative years they are frequent and repetitive enough for Monique to form a Complex. This Complex combines 'failing to do well' with 'belonging with/pleasing her parents'; it also goes on to form the (very influential) thought that 'Failures belong'. Thus, when Monique reaches adulthood, she has no aspirations and is drifting through life. The Complex formed during Monique's childhood is now, as an adult, directing all her decisions about her present and future – with complete disregard for what Monique may visibly think about the result of these decisions.

Monique hasn't arrived at this way of thinking awarely, rather this thought pattern invisibly established itself in her Consciousness. The result is that it never even occurs to Monique to apply for a promotion at work.

Monique's example shows you how Complexes work without us noticing them, be it tying our shoelaces, driving for hours while wondering if we left the gas on, or thinking that life is pointless because no one wants us to succeed.

If we don't know how Complexes are affecting our wellbeing, we can just be left with the suffering they cause.

But!

Aha! There's more!

Once we know there is a reason for these patterns of behaviour in our lives, we can stop blaming ourselves or others and, instead, know (together with using some effective tools, which this book is here to provide) that we can change them and get closer to the life that we really want.

How's your Layer of Visible Thinking doing?

By recognising what Complexes are, and hopefully seeing some of your own, you will have already started to weaken the impact they have on your life.

Do you see that you are closer to knowing *Why You Think The Way You Do*?

Now, let's get even closer

EXERCISE 2

Sit with a friend and find a random book or magazine. Take it in turns to read out a word (nouns in particular, but other words will also work), pausing after each to discuss the Affinities each of you have to that word.

Notice how your Affinities to words/thoughts are individual to you.

Chapter Three
Events

Harry arrives home from school. He walks into the living room where his parents are sitting and is struck by the thought that they are different to how they usually are. It's as though something had just happened. Harry's parents don't say anything out of the ordinary when he walks in, but there is definitely something unusual about them.

You have likely had similar experiences. Perhaps you've walked into the office at work and noticed an 'atmosphere' or you phoned a friend and they seemed distracted by something.

In all these situations, the people you observed were having or had just had an Event. Events happen to us all the time; some are simply more noticeable or have a greater impact on us than others. In the case of Harry's parents, his father had been made redundant that day and he had just broken the news to his wife. Seconds prior to Harry entering the house they had been discussing whether to tell Harry, who was in the middle of some important exams. As the expression goes, 'You could have cut the atmosphere with a knife' – there was no denying that an Event had taken place.

What is an Event?

Let's say you are strolling down a main street, and you see a man slumped over the steering wheel of an erratically parked car which has its bumper smashed in. There are people milling around and you can hear an ambulance siren.

Would this be an Event?

Yes.

Why?

Because it doesn't happen every day.

An Event is something unusual, something that makes you think much more about 'it' than other things. Eric Berne, the creator of *Transactional Analysis,* defined an Event as "Anything that intensifies my thinking"[2].

Now, if you are to carry on with your stroll down that same main street and 15 minutes later you hear another siren, which invokes the memory of the accident-aftermath that you just witnessed, could you say that you were still under that same Event?

Yes, because even though you are no longer amid the same physical circumstances, the same intensified thoughts have been triggered.

Now, consider the paramedic in the ambulance who has been called to help at the scene of this accident. Would the incident be an Event for him or her?

No, because this is a job they do every day. They see the repercussions of accidents regularly. This paramedic may have already seen a couple of accidents on this day and is in part thinking about how many hours are left until the end of the shift.

These examples demonstrate that Events, *all* Events, are not the changes in our physical world, but our *thinking about* the changes. What takes place in the physical world is simply a 'Happening'.

So, if Events are not changes in the physical world, then Events are not 'something that intensifies my thinking', Events are the 'intensified thinking itself'.

Event
Intensified thinking itself

Moving away from car accidents...
You are at home, sitting in your lounge reading a newspaper with your legs stretched out in front of you. It's a warm, sunny day and the warmth has filled the room. Your cat strolls past, running the length of her body along one of your feet as she walks to her favourite spot on days like this. Suddenly, a brick crashes through the window! The cat screeches and disappears out of the room. Meanwhile the brick hovers for a moment, then circles your head and flies back out the window. In this moment, the thoughts running through your head could be:

'What just happened?'
'Did that really happen?'
'Where did the brick come from?'
'How did it get to my window?'
'All the shattered glass!!'
'How's the cat?'
'Where's the cat?'
'Am I cut?'

These are a lot of thoughts and they take a lot of effort to process.

The answers to your questions don't come immediately, because you don't often think this number of these types of thoughts. After all, you don't often have this type of Event!

The bigger or more unusual the Event, the greater the intensity of thinking. The greater the intensity of thinking, the greater the energy, capacity and time is required to process the greater number of thoughts.

Now let's make a few adjustments to the last example...

Imagine your father is a magician and you have grown up with frequent weird and wonderful things taking place in your home. For the last two months, Dad has been practicing his 'flying brick' routine at about the same time every day. Today, pretty much to clockwork, a brick flies in through the window – which you have learned to keep open – it circles your head and then flies out again. In this case the flying brick wouldn't be an Event, it would be the Circumstance. Circumstances are Happenings which are mundane, experienced on a regular basis, and which are associated with very low intensity thoughts. Examples might include brushing your teeth or shaving or walking to work. We use minimum thinking to carry out these tasks.

Notice again, it's not the flying brick that's the Event, it's the *thinking about* the brick which is the Event. This means that anything can be an Event regardless of the situation. Can you see that this simple fact contradicts the generally accepted notion that our moods, problems and stresses are caused by the Happenings and Circumstances of our lives?! Happenings just happen, and Circumstances are just that. It's our *thinking about* these things that cause our moods, problems and stresses.

Events can be in the past, present or future. Consider the Event of my mother's death; my mother died two weeks ago, so this Event is obviously in the past. However, I could be under the influence of the same Event in the present if I'm now sitting at her hospital bedside having just heard some 'serious news' from the Doctor. Equally, this Event could be in the future, because I'm working on my detailed plan to murder her for my inheritance! Each of the Events would be described as 'My mother's death', only notice how the place in time is different – each accompanied by different impressions or Affinities.

Next, imagine that you received a letter this morning telling you that a week from today you have an interview for an exciting new job. From the moment you read the letter, to the moment that you open the door to the interview room, your intensity of thinking gradually increases as you contemplate the interview. Your mind starts to run through thoughts about how the Event will take place... how will the interview go... what the room may look like... who might be there... what will you wear... what will you ask etc. All these thoughts will appear to you as made-up pictures of how you imagine the Event will take place. This is called the Anticipation.

Anticipation
An increasing intensity of thinking in
imaginary pictures and impressions

The Event then takes place.
An Event in the present.
Then the Event is over.

Figure 3.1 Anticipation and Dissipation

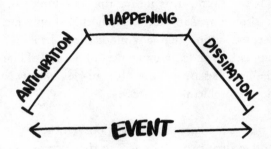

The period after an Event is called the Dissipation. This is where you go over what just happened to see what you think about it, and you keep thinking about it until it isn't an Event anymore. When it's no longer an Event it becomes a 'Circumstance'.

Dissipation
A decreasing intensity of thinking in real but interpreted pictures and impressions

Notice, that before walking into the interview room you didn't know what the room was going to look like, who would be attending, what they would be wearing or what they would say or do.

After the Event, however, you know all these things.

But what you don't know is what they thought.

This, you interpret.

'Interpret' because what you think occurred might not really be what took place.

Does this example ring a bell?

Can you remember 'interpreting' Events after they happened?

Taking our example further…

When you finish your interview, you smile at the interviewer but she doesn't smile back. You interpret this to mean that she doesn't like you and it's unlikely that you were successful. Whereas instead, this woman may have been maintaining a professional approach to cover up her delight that after an exhausting day, she has finally found someone to fill the vacancy. Her thoughts have also already moved onto speaking with her colleagues about you.

She was doing one thing, but you interpreted something else.

Why is that?

In the Awareness chapter, we introduced the nature of generalised thoughts; the important thoughts we have about ourselves, people and life itself. These thoughts can be so unrelenting that they skew our perception of what is happening to us in almost every situation we are in.

For instance, can you see how having the generalised thought that 'Life is unfair' will lean you towards magnifying the negative aspects of the interview as irrefutable evidence that the interviewer didn't like you i.e. 'She didn't smile, she hates me, I paused too long before answering some questions, obviously the company are going to reject me'.

We will return to generalised thoughts in more detail later, but for now take some time to think about similar Events from your life and how you interpreted them. Could there have been an alternative version to your interpretation of what took place? Did you even find out later down the line that there *actually was* an alternative version to what you had 'interpreted'?

Remember: People have Events regardless of the circumstances – people see what they want to see.

Ivan will give us another example of how this works.

Ivan is a Russian émigré and is on a business trip. He has taken a flight which stops in a former Soviet country. While waiting for his connection, Ivan looks out onto the tarmac and sees three men talking; immediately he identifies them as KGB (Soviet secret police). Accompanying this thought is an Event: 'People are Bastards' (because his Complex to do with the KGB has been activated). Ivan is about to turn away to continue this train of thought – with all its Affinities, Complexes and memories – when he remembers what year he is in, how his life has changed and that things are different now.

Ivan decides to keep watching the men and this time, instead of seeing what he always thought about the KGB, he sees only what is happening in front of his eyes; a group of three individuals discussing general life. Looking closer, Ivan sees that the men are a little shabbily dressed and he notices hard lives etched on their faces. Ivan sees men who probably would be doing anything else in life they could, had they not been born into a similar system to the one that Ivan had once lived in. Ivan now has some sympathy for the men where before he only had contempt. He even begins to doubt that they are really KGB. What had been an Event, has dissipated to Circumstance.

Accumulated Events

Can there be an Event but no Happening?

Recall Harry's parents from the beginning of this chapter, remember how they were in a different mood than normal due to an Event. This means that they had a 'usual' mood – a state of mind – one that Harry was used to them having.

Think about your own parents. Think about when you came home from school and what you expected when you walked through the door. Reflect on how your parents (or just the one that was home) were *normally* – their habitual mood. Can you see they had one? And that this mood could be defined? Perhaps your father habitually lived under a cloud of 'Life is hard' and your mother's world was one where 'Life is a disappointment'? These are not thoughts that come and go, they are Events that are always there (albeit in the background). This doesn't mean that your parents didn't have good moods and good times, it's just that these are their general impressions of their lives, like an ongoing background noise. These are Events with no Happening

How do Events like this occur?

Here are some scenarios that Deborah recalls from childhood:

- Her Mum always moans to her about the grocery delivery never being right but she never complains when she is at the store.
- Her Dad occasionally asks about the homework she is doing, but then goes on to make inane jokes about it.
- Her uncle complains that his doctor isn't doing enough to help him but he continues to smoke 20 cigarettes a day.
- Her older brother often needs help with his schoolwork but always leaves it to the night before it is due to ask her.

Do you see that witnessing each of these examples would leave you with a general impression about people? In each of these situations, Deborah found herself witnessing someone behaving illogically; their actions made no sense to her. These, along with lots of similar instances, consequently lead Deborah to grow up thinking that 'People are stupid'.

Although each Event is relatively minor, experiencing them often means that the impressions accumulate, likes dabs of paint on an Impressionist painting – each dab building up to form a picture of the general Event 'People are Stupid'. This Event getting increasingly stronger with every subsequent, similar Event. Over time, the Event becomes so strong that it sets up permanent residence in the background of Deborah's thinking, constantly influencing how she perceives the world and people around her. In other words, she even starts looking for 'People being stupid'; looking for times when she thinks it's taking place (even when it's not) thereby ongoing, the Event continues to strengthen.

What a life?!

These are Accumulated Events. Accumulated Events are created slowly, over long periods of time. They develop invisibly from seemingly unimportant Events which build up over days, weeks, months and years, eventually creating an Event as a Mind Erosion – a thought that wants to think itself.

Accumulated Event
An Event unnoticeably created over a long period of time from a series of unimportant thoughts

Accumulated Events have no Anticipation or Dissipation; they are permanently in your head, continuously influencing your life.

Accumulated Events grow so slowly and insignificantly that they amass themselves, unnoticed, into a constant mental background noise – a little like static or a low hum. Because the process of their formation is *so* gradual, we easily become accustomed to them, to such a degree that we don't even notice them or how they are affecting our lives. However(!), it's worth noting that others can, and do, see the influence of these thoughts on us.

Take a look at how different people are perceived and notice the Event that has caused this:

Gill is described as a worrier
Event: Life is uncertain

Raj is always suspicious of other people's motives
Event: People can't be trusted

Saul always punishes himself when he gets something wrong
Event: I'm stupid

We may often say things like, "Oh that's just Raj, that's what he does", but what we mean is that there is an Event constantly at play for Raj, which is a part of his Mind Erosion.

Mindquakes

In addition to being created over a lifetime, Events can also be created in an instant.

A two-year old toddler called Jessie is in a room with an unguarded open fire. Little Jessie likes the orange wobbly thing and wants to touch it, so she moves towards the orange wobbly thing, reaches forward and WHACK! Her hand is suddenly filled with pain and Jessie's entire Consciousness is instantly full of nothing but this Event.

This is a Mindquake.

Mindquake
An Event which requires considerably more thinking effort to process than most Events

Mindquakes are massive Events of extremely high intensity regarding a single incident. During a Mindquake most, if not all, of your thinking capacity will be taken up with processing it.

Mindquakes are more extreme for children because, as part of their early-life learning, they generate much more thinking to process a single Event than adults do.

So, when Jessie burnt her finger a massive amount of thinking went into processing the Event. Because this Event took place at a time in Jessie's life when her Consciousness was easily influenced, the Mindquake made a particularly strong impression on her thinking. A potentially serious repercussion from this Event is that when Jessie grows up, this Mindquake will have been a major input into thoughts like 'Life is uncertain... unpredictable... (or even) frightening'.

Examples of highly impactful Mindquakes for adults are: winning the lottery, the death of a loved one, walking in on your long-time lover in bed with your best friend, giving birth or the first time you see a thought that has detrimentally been running your life.

Events and Unfinished Thinking

As you become more aware of your Mind Erosions, increase your Awareness and see more thoughts emerge into your Layer of Visible Thinking, you will also recognise the origins of many of these thoughts. You may be surprised to see that there are many Events from your childhood that you haven't stopped thinking about since they happened. The reason for this, is that although at the time you thought about the Event for a while, for some reason the Event never became Circumstance, it remained 'Unfinished Thinking' (UT) instead.

We tend to brush off the importance of long-since passed Events by saying something like, "Oh, but it happened so long ago", and yet this doesn't negate the influence the Event has had on our thinking and the fact that this Event is still lingering.

Often an Event will have taken place in our early childhood which, back then, we didn't understand or it caused us fear. Anna is five years old and, unnoticed, she sees her parents having sex. Anna's impression is that her father is hurting her mother.

How can Anna deal with this?
That is the very point – she can't.
Being so young, Anna doesn't have the intellectual or emotional intelligence to do so. The experience is too confusing and frightening and the answers to any questions she may have are too unknown and alarming for her to process. And so, the Event just gets left – unfinished.

Without the knowledge, experience or guidance from elders to help us think through (Afterburn is a subject we will come to) childhood Events like these, they do not get cleared up. Consequently, we never stop thinking about these Events – visibly, invisibly or both. Instead, we develop 'coping' mechanisms to survive having these thoughts.

Unfinished Thinking
Thoughts interrupted by fear

Unfinished Thinking sits in our minds as a constant background noise. Over time our perception of this background noise dulls, and eventually we don't notice the Unfinished Thinking being there; analogous to feeling and then not feeling our clothes as we get dressed. At the time of climbing into our jeans and pulling on a T-shirt we feel the fabric and its texture. Then, within a minute, thoughts of feeling the clothing's material have gone even though the clothes are still on us. Clothes, of course, cause us no problems, but Unfinished Thoughts do.

Anna's impression of her world changed forever after the Event described above. She was left with the thought that men are abusive and that, as a woman, she was vulnerable. Not long after the experience, life started to become 'frightening' and relationships 'difficult' and continued in this vein, only getting more so as Anna got older. Experiences like this one create mental background noise that interferes with our lives. To rectify this, we should revisit these Unfinished Thoughts and think them through them until they are simply Circumstances and no longer Events.

(Note: The way that Anna perceived and interpreted what she walked in on was individual to her. Another child could have witnessed the same Event and thought that Mummy and Daddy are playing a game, leaving them with different influential thoughts.)

'Afterburning' an Event is how we do this. This involves awarely thinking through the thoughts that, as a child, we were unable to. To Afterburn, you need to look back at the Event to analyse what happened, what you thought and the implications that these thoughts have had on your life. Afterburning will be thoroughly explained in the 'Finishing Off Thinking' chapter in Part Two.

When thoughts are Finished-off, their background noise disappears and they stop affecting our ability to process and choose other thoughts. We are finally free of this incessant, unwanted, unaware influence on our lives. This resolution is accompanied by the feeling that our heads are clearer and lighter, and so are our lives.

***

Maybe some of the thoughts or memories that have started surfacing for you are difficult or uncomfortable to think about. Do always remember that no matter how big or seemingly important or influential or frightening an Event may be – it is all JUST THINKING.

To briefly summarise: Simply because you think a thought doesn't mean it is the truth.

Just because there is neuronal firing, chemicals being released and activity taking place in your brain, *does not* mean that what you think about what is happening to you is the reality. Nor does it mean that this thinking cannot be undone. At this stage of the book, do your best to slow down your thinking and remind yourself of these last two paragraphs.

What happens to us in our lives is just what happens – it's what we think about it that matters. And what we *think*, we can *change*.

Chapter Four
Purposes

We all do things differently.

One person might exercise daily, while another will sit on the couch for hours and barely change position.

At parties, one person might lean against a wall all night waiting for someone to talk to them, while another could be in the middle of the dance floor shaking their stuff.

Why are we all different?

Well, it's a matter of personality.

But what are the components of personality?

What dictates these differences?

At the core of the answer to both these questions is the fact that we all want different things.

Let's look at this more closely...

Why do we do anything in life? It must be because we want something from what we're doing. The nature of animals is to only do things that result in getting something; be it food, sex, rest, survival... and in that respect, we are no different. Humans, however, are also driven by other 'wants', and what makes human life so interesting is the variety and combination of these 'wants'.

There are some things that we all (or most of us) want, like we largely all want to belong or be loved.

But do we all want to be rich for instance?
No.
Many may say they do, but if you are not doing anything to achieve 'being rich', you can't *really* want it. To 'want to be rich' you must have the behaviour of someone who wants to be rich. You have to be doing definite things to get rich, otherwise it is just a dream.

We are talking about the drive to achieve certain things. What is it that makes us *do* things. Why get up in the morning? Go for a run? Visit family? Fill out a tax form? Whatever your answers are, it's this thinking that makes you do things – this thinking we call Purposes.

Purposes dictate our choices. If I want to be rich, I would decide to become a lawyer or a property developer rather than a librarian or a dog-walker. I could also choose to become an actor or a singer, a profession where I *might* become rich. But given that most actors and singers wait on tables to pay their bills, wanting to be rich wouldn't be my true Purpose for choosing these professions.

Purposes are a constant factor in our lives because there is never a time when we don't want something, even if it is just to relax or to pass the time. We always have a Purpose, and when one Purpose is nearly achieved the next is forming.

Purposes aren't things like 'I want the latest phone'. Purposes are *what we think we will be* by having the latest phone, like 'being admired... special... successful'. This is what we really want. The *thing* is just a means of achieving it.

Purposes make us do things. For instance, with the Purpose 'I want to be admired' I will buy certain clothes rather than others, I will stand in a partic-ular way and I will say things that I think will impress others. If, however, my Purpose is 'I want to be cared for', I will often make myself a little helpless, so that someone has to step in and help (care for) me. If my Purpose is 'I want to be special', what I say and how I do things will emphasise aspects of my life that I believe are unique.

At the party mentioned earlier, the person leaning against the wall waiting to be approached probably has the Purpose 'I want to be secure' (and so avoids doing anything that may result in an unpleasant Event). The person dancing may have the Purpose 'I want to be centre of attention' or 'I want to enjoy my time'. Purposes are what most clearly define our personalities.

Purpose
What I think will make me happy

What does it mean when we say we know someone well?

It means that we know their personality; how they present themselves to the outside world and how they will behave in hypothetical situations. This means they follow patterns that we recognise, which in turn means they have Purposes that we unawarely recognise.

Across the globe there are numerous Purposes that all humans share but we each have our own slightly different version of them. Take one of the most common Purposes, 'I want to be loved'. We all want to be loved. If you or I, let alone an Eskimo or Amazonian tribal chief, were to describe the physical and mental sensations that accompany this Purpose, the descriptions would probably be very similar. However, there are infinite permutations and combinations of pictures that an individual can have regarding how they want to achieve their Purpose.

Most of us have Purposes like 'I want to be loved' or 'I want to belong', but there are also Purposes that some people have and other people don't, or don't have as much.

Purposes and their variety, the degree to which we have them and the unique pictures we have for achieving them are what create our distinctive personalities.

In Appendix One you will find a list of defined Purposes. Don't ignore them just because they are in a long list. Have a read through them, taking your time.

....

EXERCISE 3

Discuss with a friend what mutual friends would do in various hypothetical situations and see if you (more or less) agree.

Next, given your answers to the above, try to work out what Purposes that mutual friend uses.

....

You can go to the list of Purposes now or later, remembering that you can always dip back into them (which we highly recommend to continue increasing your Awareness). The definitions will help you precisely pin down what your Purposes are and what you do to achieve them. Working with this list is a great way of understanding behaviours that result from your thinking. You may find some of the definitions confusing or funny, they may even provoke your irritation or anger, and this is a good thing. Look out for the ones that do – it means that these Purposes are probably important to you.

OK, next question. It's a strange one but here goes: How does your brain know what you want? Why is it that signals are sent for one Purpose rather than another?

If we consider that our brains are designed to actuate our ideas of happiness, how does it know whether to go to the gym or to turn to the sports channel?

How does it know whether to ask the waiter for a coffee or to kick him in the groin?

How do we know what we want?

We know what we want because we have a mental picture or impression of it in our minds. Or put more simply, if we end up kicking a waiter in the groin it's because we had a picture/impression of doing so.

You may not have noticed, but if you slow down your thinking, you will recognise occasions when these pictures and impressions have appeared to you. Perhaps you saw the flash of a cup of coffee, with the impression of its taste and smell moments before you decide to turn into the road of your favourite café... Or you are prompted by thoughts of rest, relaxation, the heat of the sun on your body and the sound of the waves as you step into a travel agency. If we want that coffee we have a mental picture of it, plus an impression of its taste, its smell... If we want a holiday, we see pictures of blue skies, tavernas, an impression of the sun on our skin, the waft of sun tan lotion, an impression of having no responsibilities... If we want to lose ourselves, we might have a picture of a cream cake or a chocolate bar and the impression of its taste taking up all our attention... And if we want to be important, we have pictures of others having some fear of us which allows us to do what we want, or have something done the way we want it. These mental pictures and impressions tell us what we want in life. The more pictures we have and/or the stronger the impressions, the more we want to achieve that thing.

Sports psychologists will tell you that a way to achieve goals is to visualise them – because this is the natural process of developing or strengthening the Purpose to do something. We see the picture first.

The thing is, we don't usually notice these pictures because most of the workings of our Consciousness have been invisible to us – up until now! All we may have noticed are vague impressions. But when we look closer at these impressions we start to see that they are made up of a collection of pictures from our past that have merged to form notions of... what it is for us to feel 'superior'... or 'have peace of mind'... or to 'lose ourselves'. These pictures and/or impressions are continuously informing our brains what to do, what to think and how to live.

Why do we have Purposes?

Well, without them we would die of hunger!

However, there is a function for Purposes apart from those associated with physical survival.

It is human nature, as almost anyone will tell you, to want something more or better, something different or more comfortable, tastier or healthier, faster or smaller, or more admirable. The Purpose of a Purpose is to improve our lives. From the moment we come into being until the moment we die, we are always in the process of attempting to get something that we want, which we 'think' will improve our lives.

This was fine when we were animals or even early humans fighting for survival, but over the centuries, and particularly in the modern era, survival is not the same issue. There are countries and situations where mothers giving birth only want for their children to survive, but in most countries survival is taken for granted and happiness has become the central focus. This is a major change in human thinking. On the whole, we now *know* we can survive so our Purposes instead are concentrated on us being happy.

The thing is (and it's a big thing), today happiness can mean anything.

Anything!

This means more than you may fully realise, and to understand this better we are going to see how a Purpose is established. To do this, we first need to take a closer look at what a Purpose is.

We have said a Purpose is a want, like 'I want to be cared for', 'I want to be admired' or 'I want to be respected'. A want must also be something we think is attainable. Many people don't want to be rich because they don't *think* it's attainable. Purposes are not dreams. If you think something is unattainable and that you have no influence over ever achieving it, then it can't be a Purpose. If you buy a ticket every week, there is a remote possibility that you might win the lottery, but unless you know a way that you can rig the results, you have no control over it and therefore it remains a dream, not a Purpose. Sorry.

It must be emphasised that Purposes are always expressed in positive statements, such as 'I want...', 'I want to...', or 'I want to be...' They are never expressed in negative statements, such as 'I don't want...' This is because, at any given moment there may be many things that you don't want, yet there is always a single thing that you want more than anything else.

Every Purpose is also 'a change I want to achieve'. Put simply, you can't have a Purpose to sit down if you are already sitting down. This means that all Purposes come with obstacles i.e. you need to do something or get past something to achieve them. Otherwise you would already have what you want, the Purpose is fulfilled and therefore redundant.

We all meet with both physical and mental obstacles. If your Purpose is to walk to the door on the other side of the room, then the distance between where you are and the door is the physical obstacle that you need to overcome. Other physical obstacles include the Purpose to clean your car... to get your haircut... to stop the tap dripping.

However, most obstacles are mental. An example of a mental obstacle is wanting a pay rise and convincing your boss you are worth it. Here, the obstacle may be your boss' stern looking face because of your recent failure to be on time. Another example of a mental obstacle is when it comes to asking someone out on a date; the obstacle being the thought that you are not attractive, interesting or rich enough for them to say yes.

We can often find out what Purpose we have in any moment by asking *What is the Purpose that I am watching obstacles to?*

You're going to a party and although you are looking forward to it, you can't help but think about a friend that you recently fell out with who will be there. The obstacle to you enjoying the party is the lack of peace of mind you have about your friend. This is the obstacle to being free to 'enjoy your time' at the party, which is your Purpose.

For this book to be useful to you, you need to start looking at what your Purposes are. It will help if you have read through the list of Purposes, perhaps a few times.

What's *Really* Your Purpose?

Imagine you're at the cinema to watch a film. You choose a seat in a comfortable position where you have a clear view of the whole screen. As the film begins three tall people sit right in front of you. In this metaphor, the screen is your Purpose and, as with all Purposes, you want the best possible outcome – you want to see the entire screen. The heads and shoulders of the three tall people are the obstacles to your Purpose.

What you do, and how you think in this situation will determine whether you achieve your Purpose or not and, ultimately, how happy you are. You could make the best of the situation and watch whatever part of the screen is within your view; you will still be able to follow the film and enjoy it. Your attention will be on achieving your Purpose of watching the film rather than on the obstacle. However, if you can't stop thinking about the people in front of you, you will enjoy little of the film. In this instance, your attention is on your obstacle rather than on your Purpose.

You have probably experienced something like the cinema-screen metaphor yourself when you couldn't stop thinking about a problem you have. You may have even found your problems (the obstacles) seem to get bigger and bigger the more you think about them. The situation can even get so bad that the obstacles become all-consuming, as though the three heads are *all* you can see and there is no screen!

Alternatively, you might keep your attention on the film and find that as you become increasingly engrossed in the story-line of the movie (or in solving your problems), the heads and shoulders of the tall people seem to dissolve and become less important. Your impaired view becomes insignificant and you find yourself enjoying the film.

The point of this metaphor is that obstacles and their effect on our lives are often *what we perceive* them to be. *We* decide whether we want to watch the obstacles instead of the Purpose. *We* decide where we want to focus our attention.

Now it gets more interesting...

If a Purpose is something that we want, and what we want is recognised by our mind by the mental pictures and impressions in our attention, then, if we are focused on obstacles, at some point the obstacles become the thing we want to achieve.

You may want to read that again.

Yes, it does say that you end up wanting to achieve the obstacles!

Can you see that if your attention is on the obstacles (i.e. the people's heads at the cinema) you are filling your attention with thoughts about the obstacles rather than thoughts of enjoying the film; your attention is on '*not* achieving your Purpose'. Which means you are *choosing* to have a different Purpose, in this example it's likely to be, 'I want to be frustrated'.

"Hang on," you ask, "What do you mean 'I want to be frustrated'?! How can anyone have such a stupid Purpose?"

Well, they can and they do.

Once you understand that people's Purposes are dictated by their mental pictures and impressions (i.e. not by what they say) then anything can be a Purpose!

People can have Purposes like 'I want to fail', 'I want to be humiliated', 'I want to be hated', 'I want to provoke anger', 'I want to be a victim of circumstances'... and even 'I want to be abused'.

Once we understand that people can have any Purpose (not just the politically correct or socially acceptable ones), then we are opening our minds up to the full range of human thinking that *really* exists, and not just what we want to see.

This is when life and people become simpler to understand because you are seeing life as it really is and people as they really are. Have you ever been confused by the contradiction between what people say they want, and what they do about it? Now you will understand why. Ignore what they want you to think and look at their patterns of behaviour – and see life as it is.

When it comes to finding out someone's (and more importantly, your own) Purpose, you only need to follow the logic. If the facts point in a particular direction, towards a certain Purpose, then it probably is that Purpose.

No matter how uncomfortable it may be to acknowledge; if you find you are regularly having an Event, something that's a pattern in your life, be it being rejected… or being unsuccessful… or anything else from the list of Purposes (including the helpful ones too) it's because – you – want – to – be!

Otherwise it would not be happening.

Being rejected can happen to anyone of course, but if it's a pattern, then it's a Purpose.

Jimmy is very unhappy at work but never does anything about it. He constantly complains that his work is unrewarding, boring or uninspiring and that he feels undervalued. So why doesn't Jimmy leave? Why doesn't he do something about it? Jimmy does nothing because his mind is full of pictures of being unfulfilled at work. In other words, Jimmy's mind understands that Jimmy has the life he wants, because he's never had any pictures of doing something else, let alone any pictures of his life being fulfilled. His mind has only been engaged with how bad things are – his Purpose is *Happiness is always having a wasted life* (Purposes that start with 'Happiness is…' always refer to a long-term Purpose – we will come back to this).

Trevor grew up with guns in his house and knows very well what they can do. One day (although he knew not to), he held a live starting pistol to his head (starting pistols have no projectile but can still seriously injure or even kill you) and pulled the trigger. Trevor didn't cause himself any harm in the incident but he did say that he had no idea why he did it. Looking back at the Event, he remembered that the impression he had of his life at that time, was that it was full of despair.

Shocking though this may seem, having the Purpose 'I want to die' is perfectly possible even if the reason is invisible to the person with the Purpose.

This is why people do things that seem strange – there are invisible Purposes pulling the strings (or the trigger) – but rest assured, after enough questions there is always a reason for it.

Teresa has been working in a large department store for over 30 years. During this time she was offered promotion on numerous occasions but always turned it down. Teresa says her reason for not wanting to take a step up the career ladder is that she doesn't want the responsibility. Teresa is liked and respected at work, she has a wide range of experience, is trusted by her superiors and is more than capable of taking a supervisory role. What is Teresa afraid of?

Delving deeper into this, Teresa could see that there was more to the situation than her simply wanting to have a peaceful life (free of the extra responsibility). Teresa could see that the idea of being in charge of anything filled her with dread. Taking time to consider her past, Teresa found the memory of a time when her mother asked her to look after her younger brother so that she could go to the shops. Teresa agreed to this but while her mother was out, her brother fell, hit his head badly and was bawling. When her mother returned home she told Teresa off (even though there was nothing Teresa could have done to prevent the accident).

Reflecting on this EA, where she was put in a position of responsibility, Teresa saw the connection to why she didn't want to take a promotion. Teresa realised that her Purpose had been one of 'wanting to be undiscovered'. Thinking about her memory, Teresa realised that her mother should never have asked her (at five years old) to take responsibility for her younger brother and that her subsequent thinking about herself – wanting to be undiscovered for being stupid or inferior – was not justified.

By the way, we're not saying that anyone who is offered promotion must accept it, it's that Teresa's reasons for not accepting were invisible to her.

By objectively asking questions about a person's (or your own) past you will begin to understand how, what appear to be, 'negative' Purposes are formed. You will understand that there is logic to what you've thought was strange behaviour, and the element of confusion in your life can dissipate. Understanding rather than judging (i.e. wanting to find out rather than wanting to be superior) will change your entire attitude to life, yourself, your past and your relationships. Rather than wanting to lose yourself from the confusion of life, you'll find you want to engage in the exploration of it instead... and see where that takes you!

This will change your life immensely.

Awareness and Purposes

- Actions speak louder than words.
- Action talks, bullshit walks.
- Talk is cheap.
- He *talks* a good job (*but never does it*).

Why do these phrases exist? The phrases above exist because we all have an objective Awareness of what is true and what isn't. We 'know' when people say things that don't ring true to us; when something doesn't feel right.

What we're saying here is that a discerning objective Awareness exists in all of us, and that we were born with it.

But why don't we have this objective Awareness all the time?

Because we have not maintained it.

We left it on a shelf in our childhood and only use it now and again when it is most obvious to us, when it suits us to or when it is so obvious that it would be cringy not to.

In childhood, our Awareness exists as a guide to how our lives are developing. We don't notice this Awareness being there because it is simply a part of us. However, as we grow through childhood into adolescence and then onto adulthood, we slowly lose it. We can see this Awareness in children, when they say (even with their limited vocabulary) the most telling things or ask the 'elephant in the room' question, which all the adults are avoiding.

Why does a greater Awareness exist in childhood and not adult life?

Because children are not subject to, or restricted by, social and familial contracts.

In other words, we *learn* to be unaware, because we've seen that our Awareness caused the people closest to us to suffer when their inadequacies were pointed out. We learned that it's better to pretend that everything is OK. In addition to this, we learned that we cannot change our lives without upsetting the people close to us. Because of this we avoid acknowledging the thought that we know our lives will not be as good as they should be, by losing ourselves with television, food, alcohol, sport etc. Which leads to us 'failing' to get on with our lives.

Contracts which link 'failing' with 'belonging' continue into adult life. Looking at your various friendships, you will see that there are occasions where you accept a friend's version of Events despite your Awareness telling you otherwise. For instance, a friend says that they did or didn't do something because of this or that, and although you don't believe them you accept what they're saying all the same.

Why?

Well, you don't want to upset them.

True, but if you are a friend would you want your friend to lie to themselves (let alone you)?

No.

So, why do you allow them to?

Because there is something you get in return, and that is:

They go along with you and what you're saying, at times when their Awareness tells them otherwise.

We do these things so that we can belong; meaning we sacrifice/ignore our Awareness so as to belong with another person – because the comfort and security of belonging is so appealing.

When we break these contracts, and ruffle the established comfort and security of relationships, things can go awry. Which is why people immediately get angry when truths are spoken. And it is why phrases like 'the truth hurts' or being 'cruel to be kind' exist. People get angry in these instances because an unspoken, but agreed, contract of belonging was broken.

Our Awareness has been dormant for many years, as we said – it hasn't been maintained. It is like a muscle, a metaphorical muscle, of recognising the truth and acting on it. To give this muscle a workout we need to recognise the negative effect that Purposes like 'I want to belong' have on our Awareness, before we can do things differently for our lives to change. This is an important subject which we will return to and go deeper into in the upcoming chapters.

I want to Lose Myself

Before we move on it's useful to clarify what we mean by the Purpose 'I want to lose myself', not only because this term will come up again in the book – but because it gets used so often in all our lives. I want to lose myself means 'to partially (or totally) occupy my mind with thoughts/impressions/sensations (from euphoric to painful) to avoid thinking particular thoughts about my life'.

There are many ways to lose oneself and we each have our own preferences as to what works best for us e.g. television, music, video games, movies, gardening, chewing gum, eating cake, being busy, talking excessively, gambling, sex, reading the newspaper, smoking, drumming, being stressed, drinking alcohol, drugs, cooking, trivia, social media, sadomasochism, staring at a landscape, doing a crossword, banging ones head against a wall, stroking the cat, writing a book! reading a book!!.... Whatever it might be, if you are doing it only to avoid thinking something you don't want to look at, the Purpose is 'I want to lose myself'.

Different Types of Purposes

Purposes can be divided into different categories. For instance, someone going to a party will have a Purpose with specific pictures of what they want to achieve while they are there. These are the Purposes they want to achieve within the situation they are about to find themselves in. At a party, I could have the Purpose 'I want to be admired', with pictures of potential partners giving me second looks… and then lingering looks… Or if a friend I fell out with turns up at the party, I may then have the Purpose, 'I want to be left in peace', with pictures of my friend leaving early. At a court hearing, the defendant might have the Purpose 'I want to be the winner', with pictures of the judge nodding in agreement with their council's arguments and eventually ruling in their favour. These types of Purposes are always achieved, or not, within the circumstances.

We also have longer-term Purposes, as briefly touched on earlier with Jimmy. This is what we want to achieve in a much more generalised way (compared to the more specific *medium*-term Purposes of the previous paragraph). Even though they are general, long-term Purposes are no less important; they refer to something we repeatedly want to achieve in our lives, rather than only in a medium-term context. For example, at work I might often have the medium-term Purpose 'I want to impress' because I think impressive people are successful. I will want to impress in my everyday activities but in the longer-term, my Purpose is 'I want to succeed'. Note that the pictures that accompany this Purpose (to succeed) do not appear as clearly as the pictures for my medium-term Purpose – the previous paragraph gives you examples of these clearer pictures. Longer-term Purposes exist as vague impressions, in this case it is of having success in my life in general.

Longer-term Purposes are something we want to think we are consistently achieving, so we express longer-term Purposes as a 'Happiness is always…' e.g. 'Happiness is always succeeding' or 'Happiness is always enjoying my time' or 'Happiness is always losing myself'. The terminology will clarify which kind of Purpose we are referring to.

Purposes are also divided into *Egotistic* and *Altruistic* Purposes. These categories are not necessarily good and bad, or positive and negative. They simply refer to how we want to achieve our Purpose. However, using significantly more Egotistic Purposes in your life can make a big difference to your peace of mind.

Before we proceed, don't confuse Egotistic Purposes with being egotistical. Read the explanations below to understand how these Purposes work and what the terms mean in the context of this work.

Egotistic Purposes are thoughts you want to achieve in other people's heads, plain and simple – e.g. the Purposes 'I want to be admired', 'I want to be respected', 'I want to belong', and 'I want people to suffer'. These all require a change in other people's thinking to be achieved. Can you see that if I want to be admired by you, *I* will need *you* to admire me for me to achieve this Purpose? The problem with Egotistic Purposes, especially if you have many of them, is that what you want to achieve is in another person's head and with that, you can never know exactly how much of the Purpose you have achieved. Hence, Egotistic Purposes *always* leave you with uncertainty. People who have a lot of Egotistic Purposes (and that's all of us, although to varying degrees at different times in our lives) suffer from this uncertainty, which is due to the constant not-knowing whether or not the Purposes have been achieved – this is stressful, exhausting and time-consuming.

Altruistic Purposes are thoughts we want to achieve in our own heads. Consider them as unselfish or self-less in that they do not require other people to change *their* thoughts for *your* Purposes to be achieved. For example, 'I want to be healthy', 'I want to lose myself', 'I want to enjoy my time', and 'I want to fail'. Altruistic Purposes are not necessarily better or worse than Egotistic Purposes, but with them you always have an impression of how close you are to achieving them – because you only have your own thoughts to consider.

Purposes and Relationships

The reason we are going into so much detail in this chapter is because Purposes greatly influence our happiness and the happiness of our friends and family.

And(!) because we are usually unaware of our Purposes, they can be destructive (causing frustration, upset, despair…) without us knowing why.

Let's look at how.

Why do we like some people and dislike others? Is it because the people we like are nice and the people we don't like are horrible? If that is so, why is it that there are people (who we respect) who like the people that we don't?

If I respect my friend, why don't I like the people he or she is talking to? Is it because I have uniquely good taste (and the friend I respect can't see clearly in this moment)? Surely this would (illogically) mean that everyone has uniquely good taste in friends, as no one wants to accept that they have poor judgment. There must be something other than our 'pure' judgment – no matter how much we would like to think otherwise – that determines who we like and who we don't. Our perception must be based on something else.

If two people are having a conversation, both with the Purpose 'I want to belong', then they are probably going to get on well. They have Purposes which complement each other. If two people are talking where one has the Purpose 'I want to provoke guilt' and the other has the Purpose 'I want to suffer', then they are also likely to get on because each person's Purpose helps the other achieve theirs – thereby complementing each other. Similarly, if one person has 'I want to be needed' and the other has 'I want to be cared for', they too will get on because they both have *Complementary* Purposes'.

However...

If two people are having a conversation and both have the Purpose 'I want to be the centre of attention', then the situation is very different. Here, each person's Purpose is an obstacle to the other's because they can't both be the centre of attention. If one person has the Purpose 'I want to be special' and another has 'I want to be superior', they will likely find each other very irritating because they will each be forced to compromise the degree to which they can achieve their Purpose (it's hard to feel superior if the other wants to be seen to be unique). These are all *Contradictory* Purposes'.

These categories pinpoint why people like or dislike others. We like each other depending on whether our Purposes complement or contradict each other, not so much because of our crystalline pure sense of discernment.

Note that even when we have complimentary Purposes with another person there can be problems. Take a look at your closest friends or family, the people whose company you love the most. Don't you sometimes think that the relationships you have, even with them, could be improved if only a few little niggles and conflicts would disappear? That no matter how much you love them, life would be easier, more enjoyable and simpler if they were a little different?

Why is it that things aren't perfect even when we're relating to the people closest to us?

This is because of the uniqueness of each person's pictures. Recall how we all 'want to be cared for'? All of us do, but in different ways. Likewise, we might 'want to belong' but every one of us has unique pictures for how that belonging should happen – and this is what's at the root of how conflict (in all its degrees, shapes and sizes) arises. You and your partner want to go out and see a movie – do you want to see the same one? Not often! You both might be hungry – do you want the same type of food? It isn't that this conflict is antagonistic but it demonstrates that we are never in complete harmony with someone else. This is because our Purposes always differ from one another's, no matter how marginally.

Two lovers kiss passionately and dream of their happiness together, they talk about getting married. But(!) he imagines Sundays in the garden reading the papers, while she imagines days out with the kids. As we said, most of the time, these conflicts are not antagonistic and are easily resolved with communication, understanding and empathy. However, the differing pictures to each person's Purposes *is* often the source of people's relationship problems, especially with their partners.

Living with your partner can mean spending a substantial amount of time with them, which can mean that the smallest personal molehill of differing preferences can become damaging mountains of single-mindedness – simply because you each see your futures differently. The make or break in a relationship usually comes down to how greatly your pictures differ. How important (or rigid) are your pictures concerning the future, weighed up against where the greater 'happiness' (and watch how you define happiness) lies? Is staying faithful to your pictures of what life... love... the future... and the partnership should be, more important to you than staying with the person that you are with?

On this subject, we should look at another reason why people like or dislike each other. We'll now be looking more closely at layers of thinking that we all have. You may have a Purpose, but there is often another thought underlying that Purpose.

Trey and Sarah work in the same office and both have the Purpose 'I want to impress'. However, underlying their wanting to impress is a generalised thought that they both have and it is shameful to each of them, it is ' I am worthless'. We will look at thoughts involving shame in detail in later chapters. For now, simply recognise that people who think shameful thoughts like 'I am worthless' want to cover this up in some way.

Trey and Sarah share the same shameful thought but the way they each cover it up – by achieving the Purpose 'I want to impress'– is very different. Trey is very competitive and likes to achieve clear results (a good cover for being worthless), he also usually dresses in a scruffy way. Sarah is smart looking (her effective cover for being worthless) but is happy to just *appear* to get results (in fact, getting results doesn't matter to her as much as looking the part). Trey 'impresses' by being successful and appearing laid-back. Sarah 'impresses' by looking and seeming to be successful. Trey thinks Sarah is an uptight fake and Sarah thinks Trey is a scruffy control freak.

So, although they have thoughts in common, they hate each other because their individual ways of covering up their issues/problems/shameful thoughts irritates the other.

This is nearly always true of the people we dislike – including you and the people you dislike.

You may want to pause a moment and take in that last paragraph again… it can be convenient to forget this.

Why dislike someone?

If we don't like the way they live, then the worst we would think is that we disapprove of how they live; but to literally *dislike* someone means something is personal. They've never done anything to us so why do we dislike them!?

What's 'personal' is that we have shameful thoughts that are similar to theirs, and what irks us is the way the other person covers it up – because it's not how we would do it. We all tend to think that the way *we* do things is the right way and, in this context, we view the way that others cover up the same shame as ours is transparent and looks fake. This subsequently provokes our irritation and even our anger!

This is why the people we like are those we have thoughts in common with. In this case, we *approve* of the way in which they behave as it is close to how we behave.

The people we don't have thinking in common with we hardly ever think about and barely even notice.

Celebrities are a good example of this phenomenon because for most of us they are people we hear a lot about but don't know personally. Have you noticed that there are some celebrities you like and some you don't and that you are often drawn to reading about them (to like or dislike). And while all this is going on, there are numerous celebrities you don't think about at all. The ones we like, we have some thinking in common with and we approve of the way they go about their lives. The ones we don't like we equally have thinking in common with but we don't approve of how they live their lives; they are not 'right'. Though, if you were to closely examine the justification for your argument, you would find it pretty tenuous.

And what about the celebrities we don't think about at all? Well, we have no or very little thinking in common with them, that's why we don't think about them.

Purposes can also distort our view of life. If, for instance, you have the Purpose 'I want to find out', then the way you see life will be very close to how it is because the nature of this Purpose is, as it says, to find out. With this Purpose, life and people are a source of fascination. However, if you deviate from this Purpose too much, your view of life becomes distorted. Contrast 'I want to find out' with the Purpose 'I want to be the winner'. With 'I want to be the winner', people are not fascinating but competition and life is a constant, never-ending tournament. Other examples of distortions (from seeing life as it is) are the Purpose 'I want to have a hard life'; here, people become a burden and life is a chore. With the Purpose 'I want to be secure', life frequently feels uncertain and people unpredictable.

Each Purpose is like a different pair of glasses, changing the way we see the world around us. That is why it is essential, if you are to become aware, that you examine your Purposes.

Read the list of Purposes and their definitions in Appendix One and start to recognise which Purposes you have and see them working in your everyday life.

When you ask yourself 'Why?...' you have a certain Purpose, '...in this moment', '...with a certain person' or '... always in a particular situation', you will be having the Purpose 'I want to find out'. 'I want to find out' should become your best friend because it lifts any glasses you might be wearing, up and off your head... to see what is really going on!

EXERCISE 4

This one takes a little courage but can be very rewarding. Pick a friend you trust, someone who you know will share their thoughts as you ask them to, someone with whom you don't have any history of falling out or grudges being held. Ask your friend: "What do people say about me when I am not around? What comments do people tend to make?"

Yes, this can be a bit daunting but take the plunge!

Notice your reactions... remember *it's all just thinking.* You are exploring your patterns of thinking/behavior. You're looking for recurring themes because these indicate patterns of thinking and point towards frequently-used Purposes. If you find this beneficial you can go further and ask other people the same question – what have you got to lose?!

Now let's have a look at how your Purposes turned out to be so different from everyone else's.

Chapter Five
The Formation of Consciousness

Why *do* you think the way you do?

How did you become who you are?

Have you ever considered how your personality was formed?

And how much say you think you had in it?

To some people these may seem like strange questions – they might respond with: "I don't think about things like that" or others may answer, perhaps irritated with this probing: "My personality is my own" or "Of course I had a say in who I am!".

It's easy to say that we are who we are because that is...well...who we are!

But is this really the case?

Do you really remember choosing how to live?

Or is it more that you remember Events... Happenings... Circumstances... good times... bad times, and perhaps you have a notion that in some way all of this affected who you have become?

It may be that sometimes something took place and you awarely decided, 'I'm not going to do that again' or 'From now on this is what I will do'. But occasions like these, when you awarely decided how things were going to be (meaning how you were going to think from here on) are usually rare. Instead, as adults, we find ourselves with characters that were formed because of a lot of unaware thinking.

In other words, how our personalities were formed was mostly out of our hands; things happened to us... and the resulting unaware process created who we are.

Scary thought?

It doesn't have to be.

What's done is done.

Here's a good question to move on with: How much say would you like to have in the *re*-Formation of your Consciousness?
Now there's a thought to work with!

The more aware you are of how your Consciousness works and how it got to be as it is, the more say you will have in your life. By reading this book, memories of how you've lived and thoughts about how you live will have started to ask for your attention, so a process is already underway. The further we tease out the processes of how we came to be who we are, the closer we are to taking huge strides in the changes needed to live how we want to live.

Sound good?

And this time you'll be having your say in the whole process.

Even better!

Nature and/or Nurture?

There continues the ancient debate between nature and nurture – are we born with certain thinking or is it conditioned over time?

Evidently there are influences from both nature and nurture, the answer isn't black or white. It's reasonable to consider that like animals, we have some innate thinking. No one told the newly hatched cuckoo (laid in another bird's nest) to push the other unhatched eggs out of the nest to survive, but they do. From birth, baby cuckoos know that this is what they must do. Likewise, humans have their innate behaviours.

The role of nurture is reflected in the sizeable libraries of psychological, behavioural, biological and social research that look at the effect of the social environment upon rearing the young. Whether the child is picked up or not… whether their environment is enriched or not… whether the child is kept with the mother or separated… whether one or both parents drink alcohol/smoke/take drugs/are refugees of war – are just grains of sand on the beach of research exploring this subject. Increasingly, it's becoming undeniable that nurture's role is critical in who we become. And this has been repeatedly recognised in the lengthy and in-depth discussions had with students of *The Science of Acting*, colleagues, friends and family (let alone our own self-reflections) about what took place in our early years. American Neuroscientist James Fallon's work on brain-scanning criminally psychopathic inmates led him to discover that he had the same brain scan pattern as the men he was researching. According to Fallon, the reason he became a scientist and not an inmate was because he had a particularly nurturing childhood.[3]

To start at the beginning…

As children we know very little. As a baby we know nothing, other than we want to survive and to do this we need to be taught everything. Therefore, Nature has designed us to learn from the older people in charge of us, just as animals do. And yet looking at the world around us, humans differ tremendously from the animal kingdom because humans have a multitude of ways to live, including a multitude of dysfunctional ways. Because of this, some of the points of reference we've learned are not as useful as others, so to fully understand the thinking we have, we first need to understand the way in which it was taken on board.

In this chapter, we are going to look at the processes which are the most important influences on the lifelong Formation of Consciousness. *Lifelong* because we are always forming who we are – that's why you are reading this book. In particular, this chapter is to help you recognise the patterns of thinking that were established in childhood which are relentlessly overriding any adult attempts to improve the direction of your life.

Unfortunately, there are more processes than space will allow us to include, and perhaps in a later publication (or by attending a workshop) we can cover the remaining subjects with you. For this reason, we will focus on covering what we consider the most important influences on your Consciousness. Rest assured that by the end of this chapter you will have more than enough food for thought and tools to support your understanding of how 'you' came about.

First, a look at what you were born with.

The Natural Frame of Reference

When we're born, we have the innate Purpose 'I want to survive'.

How do we know this?

We breathe.
We breathe to survive.

This is the sign of a Purpose. We are doing something to achieve a need. We breathe so that we can survive and we cry so that our mother will feed us... again, so that we can survive.

Nobody teaches us to cry or to breathe or to suckle or open our eyes. Nor does anyone teach us to clutch the finger being offered to us. We do all these things innately. 'I want to survive' is the oldest and most important Purpose we have. You could probably define 'life' as anything which does something to survive. Wanting to survive has been on this planet since the beginning of life on earth.

As well as 'I want to survive' there are other Purposes that you were born with. These Purposes are the primary needs that you have in common with all animals and are the fundamental influences on your Formation of Consciousness. Purposes like 'I want to belong', 'I want to procreate', 'I want to be healthy' and 'I want to have a long life' are components of what we call the Natural Frame of Reference (NFR).

Here's a list of the NFR Purposes:

1. 'I want to survive'…to find a mate, procreate and to look after my offspring.
2. 'I want to be cared for'…until I'm old enough to find food for myself and to find a mate.
3. 'I want to belong'…to find a mate.
4. 'I want to procreate'…to continue the species.
5. 'I want to be healthy'…so that that the species is fit, continues to be so and so that I may have a long life to produce more/look after my offspring.
6. 'I want to have a long life'…to be able to look after my offspring and to have enough time to achieve other Purposes that will allow me to have a fulfilled life.
7. 'I want to have a fulfilled life' (or 'I want to be free')…to fully use my capabilities in line with the other NFR Purposes.
8. 'I want to enjoy my time'…to have a fulfilled life.
9. 'I want to be the winner (or others to fail)'…to stay alive and to procreate with the fittest mate so that the species is fit and continues to be so.

Perhaps this list seems rather primal, and that's the point; we've been doing the above for millions of years… whereas we've only been living as civilisations a few thousand years! We like to think of ourselves as sophisticated beings, evolving at the same rate as the (technological, political, social etc.) environment around us, and that we make choices based on our work and interests. However, in truth, we are *ultimately* governed by nature's Purposes and, as we shall see, any major (or minor for that matter) deviation from the NFR quickly affects our mental health.

The NFR is designed as a point of reference for surviving, to keep us on the right track. It has the role of a yardstick in our thinking, against which we measure the usefulness or appropriateness of all our behaviour – to monitor the way we think and live. This yardstick does not stop us from doing things but it does affect our perception of the things we do.

Smoking is a perfect illustration. One NFR Purpose is to be healthy and another is to have a long life, so from a logical point of view smoking does not make sense. Smokers know it is bad for them and, therefore, so does their

NFR. Smoking directly contradicts being healthy and the two cannot coexist within the same mind without generating a new thought (one you would have thought about yourself when you did things you knew were not good for you) – 'I am stupid'…for doing something that completely contradicts my overall Purpose of wanting to survive.

The NFR doesn't stop you smoking, but because the NFR exists, new thoughts, like 'I'm stupid', are generated and are made stronger every time you smoke (or do anything not in line with the NFR). These new thoughts, like 'I am stupid' (for smoking, eating foods that make my condition worse, having unprotected sex with a stranger, wearing the wrong shoes/clothes on an icy-cold day…), do not just sit there though, hanging around, doing nothing… they make us suffer.

Suffer?!

Yes, because each time you smoke you know you are breaking the contract you have with yourself to have a life. You don't notice this suffering as debilitating (forcing you to curl up on your sofa…clutching your head in your hands with despair…), but you may notice the suffering as an impression of neurosis about what you are doing. It can be experienced as a niggling angst, a nagging that is constantly there and goes through varying degrees of intensity, likely just before and after smoking a cigarette, or when the subject of health is brought up.

Reading this (if you smoke, say, 20 a day), you may think 'What's the big deal? I can live with that'.
And yes, you can.
And no, this isn't about getting you to stop smoking.

What we're talking about are the types of thoughts which make you suffer that you are unaware of. As individual thoughts (once or twice, here and there) they are manageable but if, let's say, you think 'I am stupid' each time you go for a cigarette, 20 times a day, seven days a week, 52 weeks a year, this thought builds up, gets stronger and less noticeable over time. And that's where the problem lies! The more you think these thoughts, the less you can see them (!)… despite how cumulative these thoughts become, and how self-destructive thoughts like 'I am stupid' are.

We call these kinds of thoughts *unawarely evolved* thoughts. These thoughts are created every time we do something that is not in line with the NFR.

The NFR is not limited to a list of Purposes. There are other measures that the NFR provides, and these are *impressions of how we should or shouldn't live.* Imagine you've just sat down to watch the television, an episode of some old show you like is on and all is fine. But! after watching one programme, then another and another there comes a time when you have the feeling that you're wasting your life. This may come as an impression that makes you feel uncomfortable, slightly guilty or perhaps even 'a bit shit' for spending your time this way. This impression is part of the NFR, as a measure of the 'use of time'.

You may notice this aspect of the NFR as the foundation of what you'd otherwise call your 'conscience'.

The NFR doesn't stop you doing things, but it does nag at you for doing things that aren't in line with it. When this nagging accumulates, it can create so much background noise as to make you suffer and lead you (if you don't listen to and act on it) to doing and thinking things to block out this noise. The section called 'I want to lose myself' in the Purposes chapter gives you examples of how we do this. In the long-term, losing yourself only makes things worse.

There's nothing wrong with listening to music, enjoying some drinks or playing the lottery now and again, unless your Purpose is to block out thoughts. If this is the case then what you are doing is repressing unwanted thoughts, which means they remain and get stronger, needing you to find evermore intense ways of losing yourself from them.

Natural Frame of Reference
Purposes and other points of reference necessary for life

Another way in which the NFR influences our conscience is by its measure of 'the social value of our thoughts and actions'.

We have always been communal animals, so what we do in relation to the good of our 'tribe' is very important. Even something as seemingly innocuous as dropping litter affects our Consciousness. We would all agree that dropping litter is unnecessary and makes our environment ugly. We know this, but we have all done it at least once in our life. What happens when we do this is that the act is measured against the NFR, and the thought *'I'm shit'* is produced. If we continue to drop litter (and do other things like this) the thought 'I'm shit', builds up and if repeated often enough it becomes a thought that is strong enough to have its own influence on our Consciousness.

Going back to Purposes, remember that they are formed by our mental pictures and impressions. It then follows through that if we start to see ourselves as being shit or stupid or whatever…we will then start to produce behaviour that confirms that this is the case.

Living in accordance with your NFR means living with less suffering, discomfort, background noise and unwanted thinking in your life.

***

The first part of this chapter has illustrated some of nature's role in your design.

Now to look at nurture's.

People in Charge

If it's true that our thinking was shaped by outside influences, then what were they and what were the most significant?

It may be no surprise to know that it was the people who were the most important to us during our upbringing who were the strongest influence. For most of us this was our parents, which means that reflecting on how our parents thought and behaved is very important to understanding how we turned out the way we did.

How did our parents influence us? Well, some of the time they did so visibly, by literally telling us what they think about life. We know this from the way we hear people say things like, "My mother always used to say…", "Well I do it that way because that's how my dad did it…". These are common influences on what has become our daily life – how we butter our toast, tie a tie, or apply makeup – but not so much on forming who we are.

The deeper you reflect on these things, the more you will notice that it's what *wasn't* directly said to us that has been the much stronger influence. Here, we are referring to certain behaviour/thinking that was used day after day, week in, week out, year after year – because this is how most thinking is formed, through *FRT*.

Bill's father regularly condescends to the women that he speaks with. Now imagine that each time Bill sees his dad do this, a small dab of paint goes on an artist's canvas in Bill's mind; the evolving painting is Bill's generalised thinking about women. Bill's dad speaks with women all the time (the lady at the local store, Bill's teacher, the neighbour…) and so these little Events keep happening, each time adding more dabs of paint to Bill's picture. With these frequently repeated experiences, the picture that forms i.e. what Bill thinks about women is 'Women are stupid'. As with all our childhoods, Bill doesn't notice this happening because it is ongoing in barely noticeable ways, accumulating over a period of years. Nevertheless, by the time Bill is an adult he has acquired the same fully-fledged thoughts as his father.

Similarly, when Bill is out with his mother, she is regularly off-hand or even rude to people, and in the same way Bill picks up his mother's thinking – 'People are inferior'.

At a time when we know very little and are hungry for points of reference, whatever our parents do/think, is a major influence. For this reason, our understanding of the world is largely formed by our parents' thinking.

There is a natural contract between parents and their offspring that has been in formation for over hundreds of thousands of years. This contract, written by nature itself, cannot be changed or reinterpreted in anyway because it's simply how things are. This contract insists that as children we can expect our parents to raise us to have fulfilled lives, and that our parents will understand that this is their duty – be they architects or crack addicts. It is the parents' job to guide the child in what to do, how to think and how to live. If, however, this contract is broken and they fail in their duty of care, then this will lead to a great deal of unwanted thoughts (for both parties).

Mina, aged four, rushes to her father to show him how she has put on her shoes all by herself and yet he barely acknowledges her, let alone her efforts. From this brief experience, Mina decides 'Life is pointless' because 'People (in fact, the most important people) are not interested in me' and if my own *father* isn't interested in what I do then perhaps 'I am worthless'.

Can a brief experience like this really set a precedent for a whole life?
Yes!
Especially if it is a very early memory – remember the importance of the EA in the Awareness chapter.

Recall the painting that was forming in Bill's mind every time he saw his Dad talk to women? Likewise, Mina's shoe incident is unlikely to have been an isolated experience (it only seemed so at the time). Rather, this was one of many similar experiences (dabs of paints) and only in this instant did the thoughts summarise themselves into (the painting of) 'Life is pointless'. Mina's example illustrates how we accumulate thinking about ourselves.

It isn't only our parents who have a strong influence on us, many of us were raised or frequently looked after by people other than our parents: step-parents, grandparents, nannies, foster parents, godparents, older siblings, orphanages etc. In this book we will tend to use the word *parents* as they are most common, but occasionally we will also refer to the phrase 'People in Charge' (or PiCs), as a reminder that we were raised by a variety of influencers. PiCs also refers to teachers, club leaders, sports team coaches, the parents of our friends etc.

Relationships – The Cog Metaphor

Imagine that your Consciousness is represented by a Cog wheel, like in a clock or piece of machinery, where your Purposes and other important thoughts are the teeth and grooves of the Cog. When we have relationships (even short-lived ones) we try to establish complimentary thinking between ourselves and the other person – this is a Mind Balance.

When this happens, our Cog tries to interlock and turn together with the other person's Cog. The more our thoughts are complementary with another person's (in the way we described complementary Purposes in the previous chapter), the easier the teeth and grooves of each of our Cogs fit together, allowing the Cogs to turn easily, reflecting how well we get on. If we don't have complementary Purposes (and other important thoughts that we will look at in the next chapter), our personalities 'clash' and jar as do the misaligned Cog teeth.

Figure 5.1 Complimentary Cogs

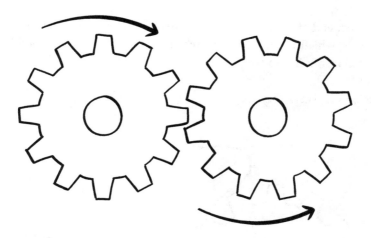

This is true of all relationships including our parents' relationship with each other. If they live together harmoniously, then they have complementary thinking and the respective Cogs rotate smoothly with the other. Every now and again there can be a little hitch, but generally they fit well together (Figure 5.1).

A baby has a very soft Consciousness. A soft Consciousness is one that is open and malleable; ready to accept the patterns of thinking needed to have a fulfilled life. A hard (or more accurately, *rigid*) Consciousness is one that has formed with well-defined teeth and grooves (the thinking has set). Aside from the NFR, a baby's Consciousness has few established thought patterns.

Extending our Cog metaphor a little, now imagine the baby's Consciousness as a soft and smooth ball of modelling clay ready to be moulded into a Cog of its own. The baby's ball of malleable Consciousness sits somewhere on top of the parents' Cogs and bounces around and around as the Cogs turn.

The ball of modelling clay never rests heavily on the two Cogs, otherwise they would deeply imprint and distort the natural shape of the child's thinking. Instead the ball just gently bobs around on top, allowing the parents' Cogs to influence (but not distort) the formation of the child's Consciousness with their own. They are literally giving the child the space to think freely for itself.

This is only one end of the spectrum, however. It's what we could describe as the ideal upbringing.

At the other end of the spectrum is a model which represents the conflict-ridden family, which is what happens when a couple with serious problems in their relationship have a baby.

Figure 5.2 Contradictory Cogs

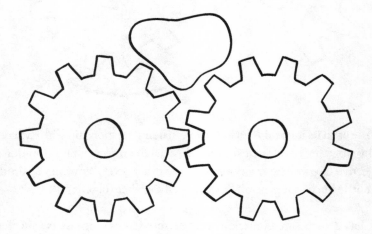

Perhaps mummy thinks that daddy has not lived up to her expectations of men (developed in childhood from her relationship with her father), and daddy thinks that mummy is not nearly as good as his mother (again, from expectations developed in childhood). In this case, when the Cogs necessary for the child's development try to turn, they jar and eventually start to pull away from each other.

These clashing Cogs mean that each parent has something missing in their life. They are together, but not really... and so they feel lonely. This will cause them to want their child to make up for this loneliness and 'bridge the gap'. This scenario can lead the mother to develop the Purpose 'I want to be needed' with her child; meaning, that if the child needs her then she has companionship and this makes her life worthwhile. The child will invisibly understand this dynamic and, in order 'to please' and 'belong' with their mother, the child develops a Purpose to complement hers. The result is that there will be times when the child does not need the mother, but feels the pressure 'to please' her. Because of this, there will be times when the child makes him/herself helpless and 'not understand' what he/she is doing, so that the mother can have the pleasure of helping and, thereby, 'be needed'.

The father also feels lonely and puts similar pressure on the child to belong with him in some way. Again, using our metaphor, this means that rather than the child's soft ball of clay being able to freely bounce on top of the parents' harmonious Cogs, it falls into the void left by their conflict. The thoughts/behaviour that result from each parent's unfulfilled need to belong causes heavy imprints on the child's mind.

Figure 5.3 Dysfunctional Cogs

Practically, this means that instead of the child simply having the Purpose to belong with their parents, they develop stronger Purposes to help the mother or father feel that *their* lives are fulfilled. Continuing our example with the mother above; the child's 'not understanding' will become the Purpose 'I want to be stupid' or '...confused' or '...helpless'. And because this is a Mind Erosion i.e. a secure path, these Purposes will eventually be there in every aspect of the person's subsequent adult life.

This is how we acquire Purposes that we might not have chosen for ourselves if we grew up freely. With these unwanted Purposes, designed only to please others, we tend to grow up with thoughts like 'My life is not my own' or 'I've sacrificed my life for others'. It is very difficult to find lasting happiness with thoughts like these as background noise.

The emphasis here is for you to look at the thoughts you developed to please and belong with your parents/PiCs. Sure, you may be sitting there think-ing that your upbringing wasn't full of conflict and this isn't relevant, but alas, you will still have been affected by your parents thinking in this way. In life, there is no such thing as a completely harmonious couple, just as there is no such thing as a completely conflict-ridden couple; every family sits somewhere in the spectrum between the two. There doesn't need to have been any obvious conflict between your parents to have developed unwanted thinking, your parents' simple need for you to belong with them was enough.

Young Edward has a great relationship with his father. They hang out together, play sports and discuss life. Edward often asks his Dad for advice and all seems to be smooth and well. There is, however, one thing that niggles Edward and that is some anger that he notices simmering in his mind that he cannot make sense of. This anger puzzles him for some time, especially as he is otherwise mild mannered. This self-questioning continues until, one day, Edward asks himself 'Why am I angry?' and his mind shows him a picture of his father.

The reason for the anger is that although Edward's parents are still married they drifted apart after he was born. Edward could see that this led him to develop a particularly close bond with his mother and resentment towards his father for not 'doing his job as a husband properly'. The belonging he developed with his father was to cover up this resentment. Even people who visibly have very good relationships can still unawarely harbour problems.

It is possible, of course, that there are people who never experienced any problems growing up. But for most of us as children, we became props for our parents' lives and our Consciousnesses have, ever-since, been caught between their Cogs to make up for the deficiencies in their lives and/or relationship. Our clay ball became deeply moulded from the teeth and grooves of each parent's Cog as we developed Purposes and patterns of thinking designed to make up for their unhappiness.

This last paragraph could be said to be a summary of how most of us typically grow up. The needs of our parents become more important to us than our own lives. We have such strong Purposes to belong with our parents (even if as adults we rarely see them) that the Purposes we developed with them continuously want to be achieved, regardless of their impact on our adult lives and/or relationships.

This doesn't mean that all parents are horrible and our lives are all terrible. It's just that these are the mechanics of our early lives, which were invisibly established. If your parents were aware of what they were doing at the time they would have stopped, right? And given many of you who are reading this are parents yourselves, this is doubly useful for you to understand. It isn't our intention to give parenting a bashing and/or to bemoan the human condition. What we do want is for you to become aware of the dynamics involved in your upbringing and its effects, so that you can make changes where you see necessary. Without knowing how your Consciousness was formed you will not be able to do this. What happened, happened. What we are interested in is what can be done about it.

Let's look at an example more closely.

Peter grew up with his parents and two sisters and all was OK... he thought. In adult life, however, he found that his relationships with the women he dated were often problematic. He noticed that women always found him 'hard to get' and he would get annoyed when they complained about his 'lack of commitment', whereas he thought that his easy-going manner was a good thing.

One particular girlfriend pointed out specific occasions where Peter lacked generosity, both financially and in spirit. He reflected on this (once he'd moved on from resenting her for pointing this out). Looking at his past relationships, he noticed that all his girlfriends were similar; they were all working class, all lacked higher education and, in general, they all lacked ambition. This fact seemed unconnected to his girlfriend's comments but also seemed important in some way. Then he started to look at the core formative influence on all our thinking about women – his mother (but also sisters and other female PiCs).

What stood out, when remembering his childhood, was that his mother regularly described daughters from other families in their community as being very 'select'. This was her choice of word, implying that these women came from a superior family. Or from another angle, his mother saw herself and her family as inferior. Again, bear in mind this is not an objective opinion, but the thinking of an individual.

Peter analysed how this had played out in his life and saw that he had invisibly 'chosen' girlfriends whose upbringing, lifestyle and profession were comfortable to his mother. In short, these girlfriends wouldn't make his mother feel awkward or cause her to suffer. Peter now understood why he had to date girls he thought were inferior to him, it was to ensure that his mother didn't suffer.

Peter, with his increasing Awareness, could see that whichever girl he was with, no matter how much he liked her, would have to be (from his perspective) inferior to him. Therefore, it clearly follows that all his thoughts towards/about them would be condescending. Compounding this, any time that Peter spent with his girlfriends reminded him of his poor choice of women (his Mind Erosion) and lack of freedom. By exploring this Complex, Peter identified why he always resented his girlfriends (even though he had chosen them), he understood why he made them suffer, and it explains the lack of generosity he had towards his current partner.

In Peter's mind, belonging with his mother was overriding any objective or neutral perspective when it came to who he dated.

When discussing Purposes, we pointed out that the basis of conflict in relationships is each person's differing pictures to their Purposes. Another root cause of conflict in relationships is the human tendency to view our parents in such a way that our partners are always secondary to them. This can be to the extent that 'through our eyes' our partners make us feel *unfaithful* to our parents.

'Pleasing' and 'belonging' with parents means different things to different people. And because of the variety of Purposes people have, Cogs with parents can, objectively speaking, be bizarre. For a moment imagine that as a child your mother seems pleased when you are being 'difficult'. Why might that be? Well, if she has the Purpose 'I want to be frustrated' she will welcome any visible excuse to fail at achieving things. You may have then developed the Purpose, 'Happiness is always provoking anger' to fit with her Cog. You make her angry, she can't get on with things, she gets frustrated – which is her idea of security – her Purpose is fulfilled and (although visibly it doesn't seem so), the two of you snugly belong in this dynamic. Although your mother's Purpose has been achieved with this Cog, the nature of it means that she also 'fails' to get on with her life and you are often inappropriately provoking people's anger.

Strange though it may seem, Purposes and Cogs like these are commonplace.

Just because you belong with someone doesn't mean the relationship is supporting either of your lives – however comfortable and cosy the relationship may be.

We will deal with how to get out of a difficult situation like Peter's in the second half of the book. For now though, it's important to recognise that while growing up we develop thinking which belongs with our parents' thinking, or at least *what we think* our parents want us to think/how they want us to behave. We develop Cogs, that is, Purposes 'to please' and 'to belong', regardless of the intrinsic dysfunctionality for both parties. Moreover, these Cogs/Purposes are not only activated when we're with our PiCs, but because:

(1) Our childhoods are perceived as the most secure times of our lives and
(2) Our Consciousness is designed to repeat learned behaviours…

…we attempt to recreate these Cogs/relationships with *whoever* we meet in our adult life (regardless of the consequences), and *especially* with our intimate/personal partners.

Pleasing and Belonging

We're going to take deeper look at how belonging can negatively affect our lives because of the overwhelming impact it has on human thinking.

At the beginning of our lives, we are born to be free. We come out of our mother's womb; we have a cry, a clean-up and we're on a clear trajectory of wanting to be free to live life to our fullest capacities!

It's a straight line from, A (birth) to B (freedom and fulfilment).

"B, here I come!"

Figure 5.4 My fulfilled life

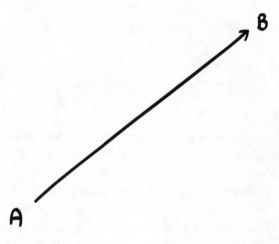

Then as we grow up, little by little, experience by experience we get pulled away from that straight line. The diversion from our 'A to B' course starts in little ways like your mother asks you to stop playing with your toys and come over and give her a cuddle. Granddad visits and asks you to stop doing what you're doing and read a story with him etc. These moments are harmless enough (and we've all had them) – but they are times when you gave up doing what you wanted to do and 'belonged'. This starts a pattern of accepting that you must forego your interests for what someone else wants.

These are such miniscule moments (which look completely harmless and can be viewed as 'beneficial' from the perspective of the PiC) and are so common place, that each time they happen we readily console ourselves: 'It doesn't matter that I've gone a little off course, I can still see B over there and I'll soon get back on track… any time now…'.

Figure 5.5 Just a little off course

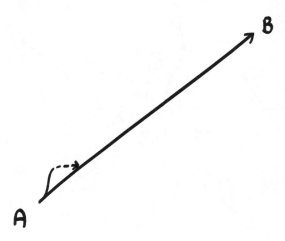

As harmless as these moments of diversion seem, the precedent they set makes us increasingly susceptible to more intrusive requests – and depending on the Purposes of our PiCs the results can range from harmless to damaging.

As we get older, the moments change in nature from foregoing our playtime to, for example, learning something more intensely than anything else (e.g.

ice skating, violin, maths etc), because other people want us to, or because "…
that's what we do in this family/culture/tradition". We don't do what fulfils
us, instead we spend time on what has become a chore and/or an obligation
– and this becomes a Mind Erosion. As we continue towards adulthood our
decisions have bigger implications, and the same precedent that was set in our
first few years now leads to us giving up Science Club (which we love) to do
Ballet (because that's what 'Mummy' did) or going to Law School (because
it's more sensible) rather than being a Stand-Up Comedian (as we've always
wanted to) or getting married at 19 (to do the right thing)… or whatever
else you may have done because you (awarely or unawarely) thought people
would prefer/expect you to – so you can continue to belong with them.

With all of this, our route towards a free and fulfilled life is now drastically
off course!

Figure 5.6 Failing to belong

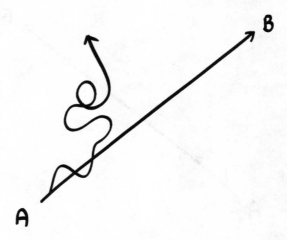

Not only are we off-course, but the path we are now living has become so
convoluted and entangled that even if B is still in sight – somewhere way off
in the distance – it feels like an enormous upheaval/struggle to get back on
track. Furthermore, making a redirection back to B at this stage involves
upsetting many people who are important to us. With such weighty obstacles, we decide to give up reaching B altogether.

All Cogs are based on past relationships with PiCs and include the Complex of failing, in some way, to belong. This is why recognising and Finishing-off the mechanics of 'belonging/failing', can and will, completely alter your life and change the relationships you have with others...

Ultimately, because you decided to change the one you have with yourself.

Which is what you decided to do when you bought this book.

Now you can re-think and redesign the Cogs which are making you fail, and instead have ones that are mutually beneficial instead.

Life is full of relationships, which means that life is full of Cogs.

What are yours?

Thought-trying-out-process

In the section above we talked about Cogs, which is the 'thinking conditioned by other people'. Now to explore the thinking we self-conditioned.

Mark notices that when he is served in shops he always ingratiates himself more than necessary. Recognising this pattern, he looks to his childhood for some clues to its origin. Mark soon sees many memories of shopping with his father, where his father would humble himself when speaking with cashiers, usually by over thanking them.

Mark noticed that it wasn't just words and behaviour that he and his father both used, it was the thinking behind them i.e. the Purpose 'I want to be liked'.

How had Mark picked this up? How did he know what he was doing? Mark doesn't remember thinking about any of this at the time, but somehow he had unawarely processed his father's thinking and behaviour, and incorporated it into his own.

Another example is Leo, who used to watch his father push food onto his fork with his thumb. Leo used to cringe when his father did this but found himself doing the exact same thing as an adult, including having the same thinking behind it.

What mental processes allow one mind to understand the thoughts of another mind? We see facial expressions, posture, hear a tone of voice, etc., but how do we *see* and *adopt* another person's thoughts...and their Purposes?!

And yet the mind can understand and copy thoughts as well as physical behaviour.

Perhaps you've watched children role-playing; acting out shop-keepers and customers, for instance? Do you remember laughing at how accurate some of their role-play was? Where did they get these beautifully-acted characters? And how were they able to impersonate so well? It's because they've had a few years of watching adults interacting and allowed the same thoughts to resonate in their Consciousness. Or, to put it another way, they (unawarely) tried out adult thinking in their heads.

As children, it seems we put adults' thoughts into our heads and 'try them out'. We watch what adults do and somehow mirror it in our heads. It is as though nature has given us a tool, perhaps to reassure us that we can become adults – that we will be able to think adult thoughts and can survive and belong in an adult world.

We call this a Thought-trying-out-process, abbreviated to T-Topping. T-Topping is another important way we learn behaviour.

Social Sway

We'll start this subsection with the question, What does it means to 'have a life'?

It's a phrase used often in society but rarely defined.

What people usually mean when they say this phrase is – having the kind of life society agrees is a 'good' one (rich, famous, successful etc.).

If this really does define 'having a life', then anyone one who is famous, rich or successful should be happy, and yet we know this isn't the case. The media, biographies and autobiographies often reveal celebrities who we once thought 'had a life' are in fact, or have been, very unhappy.

So… if what we thought was 'having a life' isn't, what is?

Ask anyone who has recovered from being very ill what recovering feels like and they will invariably say something like "Regaining my health was the most important thing in my life". Ask a new parent what it felt like when their baby was born and they'll likely say something like "It was as if nothing else mattered".

You don't get that feeling buying the latest car.

To 'have a life' means to be free to fulfil your life in accordance with your NFR. Achieving NFR Purposes (being healthy, having a long life, procreating, having peace of mind etc.) is fundamental and you will not be happy without them fulfilled no matter how much 'success' you have in other ways. And what does Social Sway have to do with us 'having a life'?

When we were children we might have had the thought that our parents didn't have enough points of reference, or the *right* points of reference, to teach us how to grow up and 'have a life'. Perhaps you have memories or impressions of this yourself?

Consequently, we decided to look outside the family to see if we could find guidance or direction there. We looked towards the people that society said 'have lives'. We saw rich and famous celebrities, sportsmen and women, and perhaps powerful politicians too. Watching them, we came up with the thought that 'Seeing as my parents can't show me how to live, if I live like these 'successful people' then I can 'have a life''.

Back then, we never stopped to consider, 'What if the people that I am look-ing up to rely on alcohol or drugs to get through their every day?... What if they have no *real* joy in their lives?... and, What if those in power are corrupt and without integrity?...'

Social Sway can come from all elements of society and not just celebrities and politicians.

Billy is growing up in a city with its fair share of social problems. His family are part of an immigrant community and are trying to make their way in a new country. Billy knows about the police and their role, and his parents' attitude towards them seems, from what they say, to be one of respect. But something doesn't sit right with him, and Billy looks outside his family for more points of reference. In Billy's general community, the attitude towards the police ranges from one of mild mistrust to outright hatred. Although Billy has never had any experiences himself that tallied with that opinion, he finds himself taking on 'hatred towards the police' as his own belief.

Even though this opinion becomes his own, it bothers him that this thought is in the background of his thinking. That was, until his mid-30s, when Billy started to question many of his thoughts and found that this one never made sense. To find out more he asked himself why he had looked outside his family for a point of reference regarding the police. With some contem-plation, Billy remembered that although his parents said the police should be respected, something didn't add up – what they said didn't match the impression behind it. Billy came to realise that it wasn't respect his parents had for the police, it was fear. And because young Billy knew that this didn't sit well with him, he had looked elsewhere for points of reference.

Thinking amongst some social groups, like in Billy's example, can lead to the thought that 'stealing is acceptable', and children who grow up in these environments can eventually think of successful criminals as 'having a life'.

Other examples of how Social Sway influences our thinking is through the media; in which television, the internet and magazines generate thoughts like 'Successful people are to be envied'... and electronic games leave us with the impression that 'Real life is a waste'… and the fashion world tells us that 'Superficial people are to be admired'.

Think about how the following may have influenced your thinking: religion, politics, fashion, economics, music, writers and their characters in fairy tales, novels, plays, films, etc.

An analogy that summarises the impact of Social Sway is that our Consciousness is a small yacht that sets off on a certain course. Whatever the initial course, a side-wind blows over from society which, because of its relentless intensity (frequent and repetitive), it can and often does, change the yacht's course forever.

Being aware of how Social Sway works; how the winds come in, from which angle and with how much force means you can adjust your sails, navigate the winds and bring yourself back on course. Bringing your Awareness to what has taken place starts the process of course-correction – and we have many helpful tools yet to cover.

Emerging Awareness

We looked at examples of Emerging Awareness in Chapter Two, and saw how the very first memories that we have, 'stick' and become a precedent that dictates our future patterns of thinking and behaviour. It's very important to consider these early memories, because early memories/EAs are the very moments when an Event took place that summarised a growing Complex of thoughts and Purposes.

Being aware of, and understanding the influence of these memories is akin to holding a rough blueprint of your Consciousness in your hands. You know what you are looking at! Because this is so important we've included another example here to encourage you to think about your own.

Sean is five years old and climbing trees in his garden. He knows there are visitors arriving soon so he climbs a tree near to where he thinks they will drive up to the house.

Sean loves climbing trees but he also thinks that the visitors will admire him if they see him up the tree, so he stays up there and waits… and waits… but as time goes on he starts to think he is being stupid and fake. But he still wants them to arrive and see him up the tree.

This seemingly inane moment shaped Sean's life by forming a Complex between enjoyable things and admiration; establishing regret at wasting his time chasing admiration. Fast-forward now and throughout Sean's adult life he enjoys his time, but he also always has an undercurrent of an Egotistic Purpose; this Purpose makes him feel stupid and a fake. The thought is that when he is supposed to be enjoying his time he is only trying to 'look good'.

Seeing this thinking made Sean feel shit and he would punish himself about it. Added to this, if Sean thinks he can't achieve this Egotistic Purpose he finds it difficult to motivate himself, no matter how worthwhile or enjoyable an opportunity might be. If he can't look good, then simply enjoying his time seems worthless.

***

The Purpose of this chapter is to show you that what happened to you as a child made a fundamental contribution to the way you live and who you are.

As adults, we think we are making decisions about the direction of our lives but unless we are aware of the workings of our Consciousness and given the tools to change, we have negligible influence on our life's path…

…a path that was paved for us in the bedrooms, bathrooms, kitchens and classrooms of our childhood.

This book is written to help you divert your paths from a future that isn't of your making, to one that is.

Chapter Six
Mindprint

"Nothing human is alien to me"
Terence[4]

Have you noticed how often people talk about the same things or repeatedly experience similar situations (at least as they recount them)? You may have experienced this with work colleagues, friends, family members or others. There's your colleague who is, once again, complaining about people. Each week this guy is either telling you about his wife, who is always messing his life up or how the boss is cutting back his hours again or how the postman hasn't delivered the mail all week! You also notice how an old friend is forever meeting guys that 'let her down' or 'treat her badly', and then there's your sibling who is continually regretting that 'things never turn out the way they hoped'.

Some experiences may even be so similar that they say, "This feels like history repeating itself…" or "This is the story of my life!". And even if they don't say these words, this is what you assimilate when they tell you about what's "just happened"… and it's all remarkably similar to what "just happened" to them the last time you met.

Do you recognise this phenomenon?

It's as though people can't help repeating patterns of behaviour or experience.

So, what's going on here?

This isn't only to do with Purposes, because all these people are talking in the past tense, about things that have recently happened to them. Yes, Purposes are the reason we have the experiences we do, but what we are looking at here is more than what people want. Notice how the intensity of revelling *after* these Events is probably as strong as their Purpose was *before* the Event – emphasising how important these Events are to the individual.

Another perspective: Have you ever thought people could avoid the experiences they repeatedly tell you about? Perhaps you've had the thought or said things like, "Well, you should have known that would happen" or "Why did you say it that way? He was bound to react as he did".

It is logical, therefore, to suppose that if someone is repeating a situation then they want it to happen, and the revelling is their enjoyment at having achieved their Purpose.

In most cases, the Events people experience are just that...Events – intensified thinking – and not necessarily a reflection of reality. You'll notice that what's common to all the above scenarios is that the individual wants to think things took place as *they* interpreted them. They don't allow space for another point of view. They glaze over, brush off, ignore, get irritable or don't even hear you when you suggest a different perspective or provide 'good' reasons why things went the way they did.

Why do they do that?

Because they have been interpreting similar situations this way for a very long time and this is their Mind Erosion at play.

What's important to understand (and to see where the same applies for yourself) is that people interpret situations in the same way as they always have, to feel secure. They regularly misinterpret reality and as strange as it seems, they want to do so! And because this thinking is invisible to them, they genuinely believe they are right.

Wanting to feel secure is at the crux of what we call the Mindprint. And we aren't referring to security as a warm cosy feeling, but rather something we are used to, something that feels familiar, comfortable, and *normal*. As discussed in the previous chapter, the security and belonging of childhood is pursued throughout adulthood. The Mindprint demonstrates how the mind perceives the way we have lived as a point of reference for how we should continue to live. With our pasts dictating our futures in this way, you can say that we actively want to have the experiences we have (more detail on this later).

In these examples and as you observe yourself and people in your life, see how we *all* have our individual perspectives of 'reality'.

You have likely experienced two people viewing the same situation differently. You and a friend see a cyclist knocked off his bike by a car and your friend blames the cyclist, which surprises you because from your perspective it was clearly the driver's fault. To you, your friend's interpretation isn't what happened… but how do you know that your interpretation isn't just what you want to think?

Clutching your head in your hands yet?

It's OK, it will become clearer

We have covered many ways in which the mind consists of thoughts which think themselves, irrespective of the immediate circumstances (e.g. Mind Erosion, Complexes, Purposes…). And how no matter what the situation is, we want to interpret things the way we always have. We call these thoughts *Important* Thoughts. Important Thoughts are Accumulated Events and the thoughts we have about people are a good example of this.

Jim has the Important Thought, 'People can't be trusted'. Walking down the street, Jim notices a man coming towards him and thinks that he appears shifty and is up to no good, whereas in fact this man just wants to ask for directions. This is how Important Thoughts work: Jim doesn't know what's going to happen but he wants to interpret the situation *his* way regardless of the circumstances…because that's what feels secure or comfortable (whereas really, it's habitual) for him.

Continuing Jim's walk down the street…
If the man walking towards him is unexpectedly prevented from approaching Jim (someone stops the man to ask the time or his attention is drawn to a billboard), Jim will walk away still having had the experience 'People can't be

trusted' because, although nothing took place to confirm this, nothing took place to contradict it either. Without anything suggesting otherwise, Jim is happily secure in his thinking that he is right about people. He will walk away still thinking that guy looked shifty and was likely 'after something'.

Here's another example: Louisa has an Important Thought that, 'Men are shit'. In this case, Louisa is always looking for evidence to prove this; essentially by putting more emphasis on times when men *fail* to live up to her standards than when they *do*.

Similarly, Johanna has a thought 'Life is a disappointment', whereby, even when she achieves what she wants to achieve, she will find something in that achievement that she is not happy about, so that she can be disappointed. Look back at the first paragraph of this chapter and see if any of these Important Thoughts could be the Events that those people were having.

Important Thoughts are also all generalised thoughts. If you remember, we've defined generalisation as a process where (over time) we summarise all our experiences regarding a particular thing, person, group of people, situation... and use that conclusion as a point of reference for how we should approach new experiences regarding a thing, person, group of people, situation...

An example of an early generalisation being formed is how a child learns about heat. Young Nikau touches a radiator and feels an unpleasant over-whelming sensation and pulls his hand away. On a subsequent occasion, Nikau is standing near the oven when his mum opens the door and heat blasts out knocking him back a step. A separate incident occurs where Nikau uses a fork to put food in his mouth, the food isn't cool enough and he imme-diately spits it out. Another time, Nikau's dad tells him how he once burnt his hand putting logs on the fire and Nikau should be very careful. These experiences, along with several more similar ones through his childhood, creates a generalised thought which Nikau will start to apply to all situations relating to heat – 'Hot things should be handled with care'.

This process of generalisation is normal, it enables us to grow and survive; it allows us to coalesce information without having to relearn it (e.g. large ani-mals with sharp teeth are dangerous). Although the process of generalisation is there to help us survive, it knows no boundaries and applies itself to any and all aspects of life, no matter how unnecessary. Yes, fire is hot and lions are dangerous but guess what...! People are all different and life is varied. But the process of generalising doesn't know this or care, it will apply itself regardless.

We all make generalisations about people; teachers, kids, bank managers, clergy, hobos, relatives...everyone! The root of prejudice lies in the generalisations we make based on the experiences we've had/heard about a 'few', which taints the thoughts we have about the 'many'. This does not excuse prejudice, but it does allow us to understand that we are all party to this pattern of thinking.

Knowing this allows us to forgive ourselves for thoughts we would prefer not to have.

In the Purposes chapter, we learned that there is a dynamic between our Purposes which cause us to have particular experiences, and our experiences which influence what our Purposes are... (Figure 6.1)

Figure 6.1 Experiences and Purposes

If we hone in on this dynamic we see that experiences also create/strengthen Mindprint Events (Life, People etc), which in turn influence our Purposes, which leads to us having certain experiences... (Figure 6.2.)

And around and around this goes.

Figure 6.2 Experiences, Purposes and Events

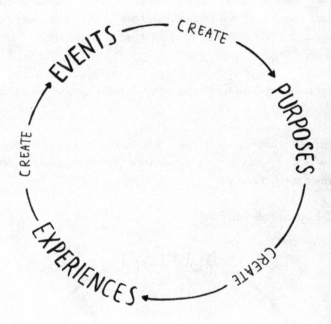

If you're anticipating a party with the important generalised thought, 'People are superior' or 'I can't belong', then your mental pictures about the party will be in the realm of 'not fitting in'. With these mental pictures filling your head, your Purpose – 'I want to be rejected' – (developed over years, from past Events) will help you achieve these pictures.

It, therefore, shouldn't be surprising that people know things will repeatedly happen to them when they say, "I told you so" or "I knew that would happen" or "There you go, didn't I say...". Well, of course it happened! They 'planned' it that way!

All of our generalised thoughts about people were formed the same way that Nikau formed his thoughts about heat – from previous direct experience or from what we were told. The catch is, we take these thoughts into *all* situations regardless of what is taking place; *believing* that, for example, '(All) Teachers want me to fail', '(All) Doctors are superior' and '(All) People are selfish'. While we *think* we judge each person on their merits and each situation on the facts, we have already decided (even before we've met them!) what people 'are' and what is going to happen.

This chain of thoughts culminates in thoughts that are both important (because we believe they are true irrespective of circumstances), and generalised (a summary of past experiences), weightily influencing completely new and unique circumstances in our present and future. And to top it all off, this thinking is (usually) invisible to us.

No wonder 'Life is confusing' (which is also an important generalised thought, by the way).

The Mindprint consists of all our important generalised invisible thoughts. In the same way that we each have unique fingerprints, we also have unique Mindprints. The Mindprint is the totality of an individual's important generalised thoughts, expressed as a list of elements. We all share thoughts about life, people, ourselves and many other things, but we each have our own unique combination and intensity of these thoughts from the range of human possibilities. This is what makes us all, and life itself, so diversely interesting.

***

First, a little warning.

Describing an individual's Consciousness using words other than those which the individual Consciousness uses is not possible. Just as Paul won't answer to 'Peter', you will not be given bread if you ask for 'cake'. No part of an individual's Consciousness will reply to a label which does not precisely fit it. In other words, if you do not use the correct name; the name that feels at home in your own personalised thinking, then the element will not fully identify itself to you. This lock and key accuracy is needed to see exactly how

109

the thoughts manifest and then decide on what action you wish to take. An example of this that you will likely recognise, is when you have a word on the tip-of-your-tongue but you can't remember it and, no matter how many synonyms you come up with, until you remember the precise word you are not satisfied. So, too, the precise label (key) must be used to explore (unlock) the specific element of the Consciousness in question.

When taking an honest look at one's thinking there's no place for being polite or politically correct. This distorts the truth and if we are not working with the truth, then this whole exercise is pointless.

As we continue with this chapter, you will see that in the main, the language our Consciousness uses is not considered socially acceptable. You may have experienced this when someone you know, who never swears, is suddenly furious about something or provoked to such an extent that they let out a rant which includes words you've never heard them use before.

Where did this come from?
Their Consciousness of course.

Often foreign nationals revert to their native language to swear when really vexed.

Some people, in these kinds of situations, will say that an expletive is necessary to fully express themselves.

The point is, if you get easily shocked, offended or hurt by rude words, watch out! The Consciousness loves these words, uses them all the time and will only respond to them because often they are the only words that fit. For this reason, one must accept that it may be necessary to use these words to communicate with the intricate workings of one's Consciousness.

To prepare you, what follows is a list of some of the most offensive words that either appear in this book from here on – or exist in your Consciousness. If you are OK with them, please read on; if not, it's time to close the book and we hope that you've benefitted from what you have learned thus far.

OK, here goes…

Shit, Whore, Bitch, Bastard, Wanker, Cunt, Dick, Asshole…

…Oh and Motherfucker.

Still there?

OK, then let's get on with it.

***

As we'll delve into in the next chapter, the process of identifying our Mindprint is the same as any other aspect of our Consciousness – we do it by gently asking questions like, 'What am I thinking about now?', 'What do I think about myself?', 'What do I think about life?', 'What do I think about people?'. This helps us to start finding our invisible thoughts, see where they originated and change them if they are not conducive to our lives.

The list that follows are the most important categories of the Mindprint.

You will notice that most categories of the Mindprint are termed 'Events'. This is to remind ourselves that these thoughts are intensified thinking in our minds and not necessarily a reflection of reality.

The Mindprint is listed in an order that is the simplest to explain. The most significant elements should become clear to you as you read.

People Events – including Men Events and Women Events
Life Events
Self Events
Shame Events
Ghosts
Adjusters
Ultimate Communion Events

1. People Events
(Including Men Events & Women Events)

Young Bradley plays for his school's football team. His father never comes to watch him no matter how many times he asks, not even when Bradley makes it to the regional finals.

Marissa's parents are very generous with her but she often feels that they would rather be doing something else. The presents she receives from them are always big and expensive but whenever she wants help with her home-work or for them to play with her, their replies are always, "I'm too busy", or "Not now darling".

John is caught smoking at school. Without taking any disciplinary action, his teacher sends a note home to his parents leaving it to them. His parents read the note but take no disciplinary action either.

What do these three examples have in common?

People don't care.

Like all children, John wants his parents to tell him what is right and wrong. He wants his parents to be interested in his wellbeing such that his smoking is a big deal to them. John may not have smoked to cause a reaction (although, this is often the case), but when he doesn't get 'a serious talking to', he can't help but think that they are not concerned about him. His parents ignoring the teacher's note left him with the thought 'People don't care'.

How about you?

Do you recognise having this thought?

It's very likely that you do as it's one of the most common People Events. It comes about when PiCs did not meet our needs as children when it was their duty to do so. This could be reneging on a promise, failing to satisfy needs like affection, or other examples of neglect – however large or small. In these situations, however mundane or traumatic, a child will recognise that an unwritten contract has been broken and often (to compound the situation) the PiCs are usually completely indifferent.

As with all thoughts in the Mindprint, this thinking is unaware and leads to other thoughts. One repercussion of having the thought 'People don't care' is that it leads to the thought, 'If people don't care about me, why should I care about them?'.

Consequently, what you do in life often becomes pointless because a grudge has built up that, 'No one cares if I do it or not', and you fail at things you could have otherwise achieved.

What you are doing is sulking with people for not caring, and you do this by not fulfilling your potential or even looking in the direction of it. It then isn't long before 'People don't care' activates the thought 'Life is a waste' and even 'I want to take revenge'.

Seem a bit extreme?
In fact, this is all very common.

People Events are the easiest thoughts in the Mindprint to identify as they are often semi-visible. If you are let down by your boyfriend on Valentine's Day, it isn't difficult to see the thought 'Men are Shit'. If your wife prangs the car on the way home from work, you may see your fleeting (or lingering) thought 'Women are Stupid'. When People Events are semi-visible to us, like in these examples, we like to think we are 'right' in thinking what we do, because the circumstances 'proved' it so. Remember though, Important Thoughts want to think themselves irrespective of the circumstances.

And now once again: Important Thoughts want to think themselves irrespective of the circumstances.

And again: This means your mind will find you the proof to believe your Important Thoughts are true.

In addition, you will have the same thoughts every time you are with your boyfriend or wife because it has become a Complex to think your People

Event whenever you are with men or women – you'll only *see* the thought though, when the intensity of the Event is strong enough.

So, although most of the time you can't see the thought, it doesn't mean it isn't there

People Events
What I think people are

On the subject of relationships, here are some common Events we have about each other:

Common thoughts men have about women are: Women are stupid, …whores
Common thoughts women have about men are: Men don't care, …are little boys
Common thoughts women have about women are: Women are competition
Common thoughts men have about men are: Men belong

Other examples of people, Men and Women Events:

People are: '…bastards', '…stupid', '…selfish', '…boring', '…vicious', '…caring', '…fascinating', '…cunts', '…have lives', '…are out to get me', '…unbearable', '…OK', '…hard to get'.

Men are: '…titillating', '…vicious', '…strong', '…cowards', '…pathetic', '…caring', '…motherfuckers', '…ungrateful', '…belong', '…cocksuckers' (thank goodness you were prepared).

Women are: '…humiliating', '…competition', '…unattainable', '…unpredictable', '…devious', '…caring', '…bitches', '…vicious', '…caring', '…necessary', '…titillating'.

2. Life Events

As with almost all generalised and Important Thoughts, the thoughts we have about life are Accumulated Events, which, because they develop over long periods of time makes them more elusive. Add to this, because we regard 'life' as a vague impression rather than something specific like an individual or a thing, it is rare to notice our thoughts about life itself. For example, we rarely curse life for letting us down, more likely we curse an individual or "That damn table!" after stubbing our toe.

To give you an example of how Life Events form, we'll use one of the most common and Dominic is going to help with this.

Dominic has a large family and as a child he repeatedly sees his mother return home with bags of shopping. He often sees her struggle with the bags up the street to their house. Dominic's father works in construction which means working long hours. Dominic's predominant memory of his father is his after-dinner collapse into the living room chair, where within minutes he is in a deep sleep.

These experiences are repeated weekly, if not daily.

We then have Dominic's relationship with his older brother, who never wants to take him swimming because he "Can't be bothered". And there is Michael, his best friend, who always wants to wait for a bus when it seems simpler to walk. These repeated snapshots, amongst others throughout Dominic's childhood, plus Events in his adulthood, all contribute to Dominic's impression of what life is. The nature of Complexes is that thoughts find connections with similar or related thoughts, so this is how all Dominic's memories contributed to a much larger and more powerful thought – 'Life is hard'.

There are, of course, times when life is genuinely hard but this is an objective thing; you can't insist that your life is hard because "Well, it just is, and if you knew my life you would understand". For instance, carrying a hod of bricks up a ladder all day is, objectively speaking, hard, while simply getting up for work in the morning isn't (sorry, we'd like to think so too.). This is an important lesson in Awareness. We naturally want to defend and preserve our understanding and perspective of life but, if we are to increase our Awareness, we have to face some...erm... hard truths.

Like all Events in the Mindprint, 'Life is hard' can have a major effect on our lives. It means that, whenever we consider doing anything at all, we weigh the opportunity against the 'effort' needed to carry it out – meaning we will often dismiss an opportunity because it seems like a burden. The harder we view life to be, the more often this will happen.

Life Events
What I think life is

There are many different Life Events, each with their own unique effect on our lives. Before getting to the list of them below, read Andrew's example of how having a specific Life Event can affect your life. This is provided so that when a Life Event from the list 'rings a bell' with you, you will have a deeper understanding of the implications of having it.

Andrew has the Life Event, 'Life is a competition'. This thought comes from the feeling he's had since being a child, that he and his siblings are in competition for their parents' attention. Although the thought originated from specific circumstances, involving individual people, Andrew's Consciousness (as it does with all people) creates an important generalised thought from his memories, meaning that, for Andrew, 'Life is competition' is activated... well... all the time! Life Events are such that Andrew lives (again, invisibly) with the idea that he is always in competition with others because he has grown up to believe that this is what life is.

This Life Event doesn't stop here. Other Events and Purposes will have been formed; you see, if 'Life is a competition' then you will have the Purpose 'I want to be the winner' which will mean you 'want other people to fail'. And, as these Purposes are part of a Complex that is activated whenever Andrew is with people, this always leads to competition, no matter how inappropriate. For instance, Andrew tends to have little arguments with friends when they have dinner together, with work colleagues he points out mistakes when it would be more suitable to find solutions, and he pushes his three-year-old son to compete, ignoring the unnecessary stress that this brings to his boy's life. Andrew also finds that, if others succeed (and people are succeeding all the time), it makes him unhappy. In these and other ways, this Life Event, together with its Complex of thoughts, causes Andrew a great deal of stress, frustration and shame.

Other examples: 'Life is…lonely', '…pointless', '…short', '…long' '…a joy', ' …fascinating', '…a duty', '…a chore', '…depressing', '…out there' '…a burden', '…a waste', '…passing me by', '…suffering', '…confusing', '…frustrating', '…unfair', '…a maze', '…disappointing'.

3. Self Events

Do you ever have thoughts or feelings about yourself that you wish you didn't? These are likely to be Self Events.

These thoughts can be created from a single experience or from EAs like the example we had of Mina, who put her shoes on by herself only for her father to reject her (i.e. 'I'm worthless'). Self Events can also be the result of an Accumulated Event.

Therese's mother has a habit of always correcting Therese or pointing out her mistakes at times when (her mother feels) Therese is making the wrong choice. The more this happens, the more Therese thinks that there is something inherently wrong with her and that she must be stupid. As these little thoughts accumulate over the course of her life, the Self Event 'I am stupid' becomes a deep ditch. Consequently, Therese can never trust anything she thinks because it could be wrong and so decision-making is very stressful; she always needs to be 100 percent sure she is right before making even the simplest or most mundane of decisions.

Therese and Andrew have illustrated how every thought, Purpose or Mindprint Event activates other thoughts, which contribute to their stress and suffering. This is no less true of Self Events.

Self Events can (with a little digging) be relatively easy to see. The hitch often lies in it being difficult to admit to ourselves, let alone others, that we think these things about ourselves. It might be cringy to admit you think you are 'special' let alone that you have the thought that you are 'inferior' or 'a failure' or 'a whore' or 'unlovable'... (remember these are all simply *thoughts* you have, which doesn't mean they reflect reality – but they *are* affecting your quality of life!). Dealing with Self Events takes some courage. You need to honestly look at and accept what you think about yourself *without judgement* for their power to weaken.

Self Events
What I think I am

We can, and do, have many different Self Events and the one that predominates depends on the Complex being activated at the time. At home with his parents, Jean has the Self Event 'I'm special' (because they always make him the centre of their lives), and at work as a music teacher he has 'I'm capable' (because his skill as a musician was nurtured by his family), whereas socially he thinks 'I'm inferior' (because his friends seem to be able to cope with all aspects of life much better than he does).

Have you noticed that sometimes you do something that you strongly regret and, on reflection, you blurt out loud to yourself something like "I'm so stupid" or "What a twit!" or "I'm such an idiot" or worse. These are examples of times when we express what we *really* think about ourselves. However, we don't tend to give these moments a second thought, thinking these are isolated thoughts – but as we have seen with Complexes, there are no isolated thoughts. This isn't to say that this applies to everyone every time they do something like this, but if you notice you have a pattern of saying certain things about yourself, then it may be for you.

A Self Event is a summarised impression of what we think about ourselves. It begins with 'I am...' plus a descriptive word.

Other examples: 'I am...inferior', '...OK, '...a little boy' (a thought that can be had by either sex), '...a little girl' (a thought that can be had by either sex), '...a stupid cunt', '...an evil genius', '...Jesus', '...my mother's fuck', '...God', '...guilty', '...lonely', '...a failure', '...a dick', '...a victim of circumstances', ' ...abandoned', '...an asshole', '...trash', '...killjoy', '...capable'.

4. Shame Events

We all do, have done or have had done to us, things that we are ashamed of. We call these Shame Events. Whatever took place may not be something we would all agree is shameful but, as we've said before, it rests on the perspective of the individual who thinks the thought – not anyone else's. Many Shame Events are visible things which took place in adult life, like stealing from a shop, secretly drinking alcohol…as well as small things like lying to a friend to avoid something or losing something you've borrowed (note again: these examples are totally subjective, what is cringy to one person isn't to another). If you look back over your adult life you will find that you've done things that made you cringe, squirm, shrink, suffer, etc. but uncomfortable as these thoughts are, they can be dealt with relatively easily so that they stop impeding the quality of your daily life.

Some Shame Events are so shameful however, that we hide the related pictures and impressions from ourselves underneath the detritus of day-to-day living. These stronger Shame Events are the ones we acquire in childhood and usually involve ourselves or our families, and often the relationship between the two. Shame Events can be about a specific Happening and/or about an Accumulated Event regarding our family's way of life. Whatever the origins, the results of Shame Events can be devastating.

Zac's parents told him that his birth had not been planned; his mother had used contraception but it failed. Zac also knew that his parents had married young. These two things (along with some problems in his parents' relationship), made Zac think that the only reason they had married was because of him and not because of the love between them or for him. This information led Zac to think he was 'unwanted' and 'unloved' and this was his major Shame Event.

Courtney is growing up in a reasonably loving family home but she can see that there are things that bother her: her parents rarely kiss, her father often forgets her mother's birthday, her mother is never 'tender' towards her father and is often wound up or frustrated when he is around, and there is regularly an air of friction in the house which both parents appear to ignore. Later in life, when Courtney reconsiders these and other niggles, her summary of it all hits her like a brick: 'My parents did not love each other'. There had never been a single Event that led Courtney to this conclusion, rather it was an accumulation of small Events. Once Courtney saw this, it made complete sense, as though she had always thought it (invisibly) but hadn't realised it (visibly).

Shame Events that originate/develop in childhood, have a huge impact on a Consciousness and, therefore, affect a person's entire life. Zac's shame of thinking he was unwanted meant that he did not want to grow up. Zac's reasoning for this was that by staying a child, there was at least a chance that he could receive the love he so craved. Whereas (he thought), if he were to accept that he was an adult, the possibility of receiving this love would be over. Zac would then also have to accept that he had never truly known what it is to have been loved/wanted. Consequently, any major developmental steps in Zac's life, like starting secondary school or puberty, were dealt with on a visible level – he superficially 'showed' the world he was older – but Zac knew he had to remain, in his mind, a little boy.

As an adult, Zac 'played the game' of being an adult whereas what he felt was that he didn't fit in and that his life is fake. In this way, his shame compromised his daily life because the decisions he made were based on his refusal to grow up, and his fear of others finding out he wasn't the man he appeared to be.

Like Zac, Courtney's Shame Event caused her problems in adult life. Courtney constantly felt insecure and that something bad was about to happen. This was rooted in the fear that her parents would split up, the same fear she had invisibly lived with throughout her childhood. It may be no surprise that Courtney lived in a permanent state of stress and anxiety.

On top of the specifics of these examples, Shame Events affect our lives in more general ways. While we have them, they bother us as background noise – liken it to having someone gently prodding you all the time. After a while this becomes unbearable and you need to numb yourself or lose yourself to avoid 'feeling it'. We all have the Purpose 'to lose ourselves' from time to time: having a drink at the end of a hard day, going on a shopping spree when feeling low, wolfing down bars of chocolate to stave off thoughts of loneliness…. These are all common manifestations of this thinking.

Shame Events make us feel we need to lose ourselves near-constantly to survive daily life. Losing ourselves soon becomes a constant fixture in our lives and becomes a part of 'who we are' – our identity. Eventually we are losing ourselves from life – so as to 'live' (very much in inverted commas).

More ingrained/deeper/stronger Shame Events cause greater levels of suffering and necessitate additional 'heavy duty' levels of losing ourselves (e.g. gambling, addictions to mind altering substances, other pathological behaviour...).

Shame Events often originate in childhood because they happen at a time when we don't have the knowledge/experience to understand the world as it is. Let's say I have a thought that my family are shameful to me... I will then have the thought that 'I am inferior', because (if I don't live with any other families to compare with how they live), I will logically believe that I am the only one with a family shameful in the way mine are. As I get older, this feeling of inferiority builds up to such an extent that even though I am old enough to know that others have had equally dysfunctional lives, the Mind Erosion is now well established. This shame is now activated whenever I am with people – which, let's face it, is most the time!

Shame Events also affect other people's lives, directly or indirectly. Remember Therese from a couple of pages ago? While Therese was growing up she never seemed to be able to do things to her mother's satisfaction, either it was the wrong decision or it was done badly, and this could be anything from performing in the school nativity play to washing the dishes. Mostly, these weren't big Events, just comments about how things could be done differently or better. However, little by little, day after day, Therese had a feeling that there was something wrong with her for her mother to keep doing this and that this must mean she was stupid. This, in time, became Therese's Shame Event – 'I am stupid'. In her everyday life, this Self Event meant Therese needed to put time and effort into covering up this (shameful) thought, so that others wouldn't see it.

When Therese compared her life to others', she felt hers was full of stress and suffering whereas all she could see was that 'Other people have lives' (very common People Event). Down the line this led Therese to want people to fail

– because if they failed, she didn't feel so bad about her life because then she wasn't the only one failing.

The above is a very common Complex and in truth, alas, we all have it. But…! Because 'wanting others to fail' is socially unacceptable, we cover it up in various ways; from simply having a blank expression, to having strong Devices (to cover the Action, 'I enjoy' when people fail), to being seen as liberal, kind-hearted, warm, generous and caring.

It must be emphasised that the people we tend to 'want to fail' the most are our friends and family. This is not because we are inherently nasty people but simply because they are in our lives the most. We can lose ourselves from the rest of the world 'getting on' but the thought of the people surrounding us having a life (all the time in front of our eyes) while we are failing, is intolerable.

Comparing 'wanting others to fail' with our NFR – the yardstick that monitors and measures the true quality of our lives – will register this Shame Event and subsequently create another Shame Event – the thought 'I am shit' (…for 'wanting others to fail').

And so life goes on…
And so our Shame Events, Life Events etc. get strengthened…

Consider the time, effort and energy that goes into maintaining and covering shameful thoughts.

Next, an example to illustrate how we indirectly make people fail because of the choices we make to cover up our shame, rather than doing what's best for them, be they families, friends or colleagues.

Tim's father Harold has the Shame Event, 'I'm shit'. Harold never talked about this thinking, mainly because it was invisible to him, but Tim pieced it together having spent 30 years living with or close to his father and having heard many of Harold's childhood stories. We won't go into why Harold has the thought 'I'm shit', instead we are looking at the repercussions of Harold's Shame Event, so that you have another example of the mechanics of this kind of thinking. So, because of Harold's shameful Self Event he feels very uncomfortable being with his son when other people are around; particularly in situations where Harold feels insecure or inferior. This means Tim's father avoided many of his son's important days, like school parent-teacher meetings, football matches and even when Tim became a successful actor, Harold never went to see his son perform, regardless of whether he was a lead role. Until Tim identified what Harold thought about himself, Tim thought his father simply 'didn't care' and if he didn't care, it must be his (Tim's) fault. By unravelling his father's shameful Self Event, Tim also understood how he had acquired his own Shame Event, 'I am worthless'. And this, you could say, evolved from his *father's* Shame Event.

Did it get past you?
Or did you question it?
Did you notice that Tim saw Harold's behaviour as his fault and not his father's responsibility?
Why would Tim think that?
Why, if you also considered it acceptable, would you?

Tim's example illustrates that, as children, none of us want to believe that the people with whom we most want to 'belong' with, the ones that mean the most to us, the ones that believe are our heroes... yes, our own parents... are making us fail. This is why it was more comfortable for Tim to think he was worthless, than it was for him to think, 'I have a shit father' (although that thought was there in the background). As a child, Tim didn't have the understanding or empathy to grasp the roots of his father's insecurities, which (of course) had nothing to do with him. They stemmed from a different context than that which Tim was seeing him in.

This deeper understanding of his relationship with his father, helped Tim objectively recognise how his *own* Shame Event 'I am worthless' had developed. Tim was then able to understand the consequences this brought into his own fatherhood.

Unless Shame Events are dealt with when they are created, they start a chain-reaction from parents to children, only for those children to become parents and create Shame Events in their offspring and so on and on. Variations of this problem are being handed down generation to generation, continuously, everywhere! If, for instance, Tim thinks he is worthless, he will see his children as being superior to him. His kids will unawarely understand this, and feel so bad about it that they will make themselves fail in some way to belong with him.

Shame Events are *the* major cause of stress, suffering and unhappiness in individuals because not only do we live with them, we have to compensate for them, hide them, and make other people suffer for them. This causes us even greater shame, guilt and suffering…

Shame Events
The thoughts that cause me the most suffering and the ones that I must hide from others and myself

In short, Shame Events create such an intricate web of unwanted thoughts that they prevent us from getting on with our lives and living fully because we have become a fly snagged in the web that Shame Events create. The same web that extends to catching our friends and family too!

By contrast, when Tim saw his father as an individual who had problematic thinking of his own, he was able to loosen a Complex which had dogged his life. He was able to see his father as a man who had his own problems (which had been handed down to him), and was able to forgive him.

***

Many people's Shame Events are experiences that can be considered abuse – whether, emotional, violent or sexual in nature they can range in severity from unpleasant to extreme. Unfortunately, this type of human experience is much more common than we may want to think.

Extreme cases of abuse, particularly when it involves celebrities or politicians, are increasingly in the media. Although these cases are now being reported more than ever, a greater majority of abusive Events go unreported (and unspoken), usually because they involve family/friends of the family.

If you've experienced anything of this nature, don't think that it can't be Finished-off because it can. Although it is possible to do this yourself, you would greatly benefit from a support group or councillor to assist you. The information and tools in this book will help you think through the Event(s) in question and explore the avenues of your life that have been affected by what has taken place. This will give you the opportunity to change the consequences that any such experience has had.

We are living in a time when subjects like childhood-abuse are becoming easier to talk about so this isn't something you should feel you need to hide away from (as we have tried not to here). You can start by using the tools in this book to Finish-off something less upsetting to show yourself that it can be done, and with that inspiration and a little courage, take the next step and reach out for help.

***

If there is one subject that should not be overlooked in this book (and will lead to the greatest personal gains) it is Shame Events; their existence, work-ings and far-reaching influence. Start looking for your own to finish them off and see your life start to dramatically improve for the better. This cannot be overstated. Try it and find out for yourself.

It may be an uncomfortable process, especially at first, but, as we keep coming back to, remember *these are just thoughts* and they do not have to rule our lives, we can deal with them rather than let them haunt our entire lives.

Speaking of haunting here's the next subject…

5. Ghosts

Imagine yourself as a child at a party where you and the other children all propose games to play but your suggestion is not chosen. From this episode you may think, 'They didn't like my idea' or maybe even, 'They don't like me' – like a little Ghoul that momentarily haunts you. Next, say at school the following week, you are the last to be chosen when teams were being picked by classmates. From this you think, 'I'm unpopular' – another Ghoul. In the playground, you walk over to a group of kids playing and they immediately disperse when they see you coming…you think, 'Was it because of me?'. Each individual Event is small but over time these little Events build up and club together to form (an Accumulated Event) a much larger thought – a Ghost. In this example, it is 'I can't belong'.

Once established, this Ghost looms large in your Consciousness whenever people are around; affecting how you live and the Purposes you use. In time, you develop Purposes of rejection and lonely life to confirm that this Ghost is real.

Ghost
A recurring fear that has the Purpose of maintaining an
unawarely favoured pattern of thinking/behaviour

Most of us have Ghosts. The Ghost 'I can't belong' is a very common one. Have you ever been at a party and had a thought that everyone else seems to 'belong' easily but you feel insecure. Well, guess what?! That's what everyone else is thinking (albeit with their own Affinities)! They may have covers and ways of dealing with this Ghost but most people have insecurities about belonging.

6. Adjusters

Kerry has what she considers to be a lonely life; she doesn't get invited out, she doesn't have many friends etc. But like all of us, Kerry's life is what she's made it, and Kerry's life is lonely because she has a Purpose to have a lonely life.

How does this Purpose work?
How did Kerry end up living the very life (she says) she doesn't want to have?

The way that the Purpose, 'I want to have a lonely life' works with Kerry is through her use of 'Adjusters'; little thoughts which pop into her head to keep her life the way she is used to it (in this case, lonely). For example, one day a work colleague invites Kerry to a party. An invitation to a party! Perfect! This is the ideal opportunity for Kerry to change her pattern of loneliness, at least for a few hours, and who knows what it could lead to. But at the moment of the invitation, a thought immediately jumps into Kerry's head, 'Oh, there's no way I could go…I'm so busy' or '…I'm too tired' or 'Parties really aren't my thing'. Kerry is given the ideal opportunity to make a small change in her life and an Adjuster pops in which steers her back to her Purpose. She makes an excuse, and doesn't go.

Notice that not only do Kerry's Adjusters ensure she 1) avoids an opportunity to belong but 2) they allow her to revel in thoughts of others enjoying their time at the party, further compounding her sense of loneliness.

Adjusters are little thoughts that pop into our thinking at the very moment when change threatens the stability of our Mind Erosion. Another example is Pepe, who dreams of having his own business but in reality he wants to fail. An opportunity arises to get involved with a new venture and immediately Pepe thinks, 'It's too good to be true' or 'It's too risky' and he rejects the idea.

Look for your Adjusters in your everyday life as they will tell you where you are failing to have a fulfilled life.

Other examples: 'It's not worth it', 'It won't work', 'It's all shit anyway', 'It's too late', 'Nobody cares anyway', 'I'll do it later', 'I can't be bothered', 'My mother wouldn't like...', 'It's different for me', 'It can't be true', 'It can't be that simple', etc.

7. Ultimate Communion Event

> *"We're all of us sentenced to solitary confine-*
> *ment inside our own skins, for life."*
> **Tennessee Williams[5]**

We do not need to take the same bleak view as Williams but there is something to what he says, in that we can never get inside the heads of another human being; we can only be in our own.

Saying that, we all very much want to 'belong', and with some people more than others. It's likely that you want to belong with your friends more than you want to belong with the postman, which means there are degrees of 'belonging'. When walking along the street, you notice a funny thing happen and turn to exchange a glance with someone who also saw it. This is a small moment of belonging with that person. At the other end of the spectrum there are times in all our lives when we have shared an incredibly strong sense of belonging with someone, someone who we feel will always be special to us. These degrees of belonging lead us to an impression of the *ultimate* belonging – belonging with someone, some people or some*thing* even, which is the closest belonging experience we could ever have and which gives us the most satisfaction; we call this the Ultimate Communion (UC).

So, who would be the entities that we most want to belong with? In most cases, it is our parents or the people who raised us – our PiCs.

From the moment we are born (and likely before), we started a lifelong relationship with our parents that is not only frequently and repetitively thought about (everyday, many times a day), but which started at a time when our Consciousness was forming. Consequently, the Complexes and impressions formed at this time are the ones we are profoundly drawn to regardless of what happens to us in later years.

Most often the UC is with one of our parents – and usually the parent of the opposite sex to us. Which leads us to the thorny subject of sex. We are born to think sexually because without sex the human race would die out. Sex is a fundamental need and because sex depends on belonging as part of its Complex, belonging in all its shapes and guises can and does include sex. Therefore, to achieve a strong sense of belonging, the belonging is unfulfilled if sex is not part of it. Although we may find the idea of sexual thoughts between us and our parents revolting, it does not mean they do not exist. Remember, we are not intellectuals who can turn off thousands, if not millions of years of programming any more than we can resist the desire to sleep. First and foremost, we are animals, and so sex is something that is fundamental to us, despite us having thoughts about it that as 'modern humans' we would rather not have.

This is not a new subject; psychotherapists have written tomes about the varied relationships we have with our parents, and again, especially with the parent of the opposite sex. Perhaps there would be more information available if we were not so frightened of what we might find! Saying that, life has many commonly understood and accepted references to this relationship; as seen in films, books, poems etc. The Electra and Oedipus Complexes are taken from Greek mythology and so if this was not part of the human condition it would have been rejected long ago. What do you think the roots of phrases like 'mummy's boy' and 'motherfucker' really are?!

We recognise that for some the UC Event may be the most contentious part of this book and, for many, difficult to take on board. But what have you got to lose by considering it? If it's true or untrue for you then you will find this out. If it isn't true (despite the decades of combined academic and personal research that have gone into writing this book), fine. If it is true, then you will have gained some knowledge that may very well set your thinking free.

And, either way – don't panic!

Sexual pictures between family members are not normally visible (though they can be), nor would we see them immediately if pointed out, nor would anything necessarily happen between the family members given an opportunity; and yes, all those who have seen their own thoughts about this have cringed out of their skin. We are simply talking about the 'want to belong' and belonging for all animals, as we've discussed, includes the Complex of sex.

Cringe.

Squirm.

Now relax – it's just thinking.

In most cases, the UC Event is an Accumulated Event. It is a summary of all the thoughts one has had about belonging with the object of their UC, including the Affinities they have acquired from that person; likes, dislikes, styles, Mindprint etc. The UC evolves throughout a person's life and even continues to develop after the person in focus has died.

Nathan's mother, Rose, has a couple of minor conditions that are not life threatening but are disabling. Rose often complains about them and lets everybody know how much she is suffering – the impression is that she enjoys talking about it. While Nathan was growing up, he developed the same conditions as Rose but these wore off in adulthood. What did not wear off though, was the impression of suffering that he shared with his mother. When he took a closer look at his thinking he could see that within the Complex of belonging with Rose, there was the thought, 'Suffering people belong' i.e. because we suffer we have something in common. If suffering people belong, then to belong there always needs to be some suffering. Because Nathan's UC is with his mother, whom (like nearly all of us) he is with almost every day of his childhood and who is probably the most important person in his life, it means that this Complex of suffering was firmly established, if not entrenched. So much so that the more suffering there is, the closer the sense of belonging. This is how UC works – it establishes Affinities and then the bearer devotedly pursues them.

The UC Event comprises thoughts and feelings from one's early years when there was a need for security and belonging with someone who, depending on what they provided (anything from care to abuse), shaped the UC to include these Affinities. It can mean the UC includes impressions of being loved, rejected, protected or humiliated…and many more possibilities.

These impressions are as varied as there are people. They can include people who are in distant geographic locations, people we haven't seen for years and even those that are no longer alive. They can involve specific or vague circumstances and can also include the impression of sexual penetration.

Ultimate Communion Event
The generalised impression of the most secure
relationship I can ever be in

Sarah has two sisters who compete for their father's attention, to such an extent that Sarah feels she can never have him to herself. This feeling is there throughout her childhood and early adult life. When Sarah analysed her thinking, she found her UC Event was with her father but she could only achieve the UC once he was dead. As strange as it may seem, Sarah's logic was that only then would she have him to herself.

The UC Event overwhelmingly affects our everyday life because the pursuit of this ultimate belonging/security is a major influence on *all of our decisions* – far beyond our immediate relationships. Nick's mother enjoys her son's wild behaviour and invisibly encourages him; 'Boys will be boys'. His father, however, disapproves and is often angry with him for behaving badly. This three-way dynamic formed the basis of countless situations of their everyday lives, and gradually built up into Nick's most secure feeling of belonging.

Nick's UC is, therefore, with both parents (because his father's disapproval, while Nick belongs with his mother, is always in Nick's head). With the UC being a Mind Erosion, Nick recreates it everywhere he goes: This plays out as Nick frequently finding himself at odds with other men; with a tendency to provoke their disappointment and anger, but all the while retaining the pride of someone who is somehow winning. 'Somehow winning' because he appears to be enjoying life even though his behaviour is often stupid/annoying and is creating stressful relationships. Each of these elements, stemming from the relationship he has with each of his parents, makes up his UC.

Do you remember Brian from the chapter on Awareness? Do you remember he didn't know why he had pushed the girl off the gym horse that day? Go back and read that bit now if you want and come back. It's at the beginning of the chapter.

As Brian's Awareness developed he began to gain more insight into why he pushed Tracy off the horse that day. When Brian understood how the UC works he was finally able to fully comprehend the core of his surprising behaviour. This is how he unravelled it: At the time in question, Brian is 11 years old and about to leave Junior School and join Secondary School; a step up the ladder of becoming a man. The closeness of his relationship with his mother makes him feel inferior to other boys who he has no reason to suspect have this same familiarity with their mothers. This strong belonging (UC!) means that Brian's mother is the primary person in his life and anyone else will automatically be second. In turn, this means that any girl who gets in the way of this bond will not be welcomed.

When Tracy began drawing attention to herself with her 'poses' on the horse, Brian began thinking about girls in a sexual way (no matter how innocently) and this made him feel 'unfaithful' to his mother. This, coupled with the underlying sense of inferiority about becoming a man, triggered enough anger in Brian to push Tracy off the horse.

The UC Event is such an integral part of an individual's Consciousness that achievement of it, however convoluted or unbelievable, is the most important goal in life, influencing every experience we have.

Having an UC with anyone other than the person we have chosen as our partner will affect this immediate relationship – how can it not? If, in our minds, we have 'decided' that X of our UC is our 'Number One', and the way of belonging with X is unique and the ultimate, how can we then adjust our thinking to suit our partner (who will of course have their own UC)?

A great deal of what we do when we look for a partner is we (unawarely) try to find someone *who will allow us* to get as close as we can in our pursuit of UC, but of course it is never perfectly aligned, and this disparity causes friction between partners.

Do note – the UC Event is one of the *least visible* elements of the Mindprint, so it may take you some time to fully digest everything in this section, see how it works and then (ultimately!) identify yours. The UC plays a principal role in influencing your life and while being the most important element of your Mindprint it is, to repeat, paradoxically the most invisible.

Mindprint
A verbal embodiment of the elements of the mind and its important, generalised and invisible thoughts

Once you identify your UC alongside your Shame Events, Life Events, People Events, Self Events etc. you will have a map of your mind's most important (because they think themselves irrespective of circumstances) generalised (because they are summaries of past experiences that are used as points of reference for present and future experiences) invisible thoughts, and thereby, a fundamental key to unravelling a considerable amount of 'unfathomables' – in your thinking and in your behaviour. In short, by identifying your unique Mindprint you will have a vastly greater understanding of *Why You Think The Way You Do*.

***

We started this chapter with the Roman playwright Terence's quote, "*Nothing human is alien to me*"[4]. This speaks of accepting that we are all the same, that none of us can exclude ourselves from any human thought and we should accept the humility and universality of this notion. We hope this chapter has demonstrated this.

This quote also implies something else, something very positive, verging on the profound; it's that if another can have thinking/behaviour which I too would like to have...

I can.

EXERCISE 5

Now that we have covered all the Mindprint elements and seen how they work, why not go through this chapter again to identify your own? You probably did this as you went along when something stood out for you and you had an Affinity towards it. Well, now go ahead and write it down.

By writing out your Mindprint you will have an aide to work with in Part Two (and when you re-read Part One), providing you with specific thoughts to explore. Use it to see how these thoughts work in your life and to see the co-existent Affinities. This will help you understand your Mindprint at a deeper level.

In time, go through the list again and notice the changes you have made in your life; you should be able to see how your Mindprint weakens with your increasing Awareness.

Chapter Seven
Actions

In Chapter Four we talked a lot about Purposes but we didn't cover *how* we achieve Purposes.

If 'I want to take revenge' on someone I might punch them in the face, whereas if 'I want to ingratiate myself' with them, I may smile and nod while they are speaking. If 'I want to be rejected' by someone, I may pick my nose in front of them, whereas, if 'I want to be cared for' by them I will show them the cut on my knee, where I fell running for a bus. These are all physical actions – physical actions taken to achieve Purposes.

Physical actions aren't the only way to achieve Purposes, especially as many Purposes don't always need a clear physical action to achieve them. A good example is lying on a beach with the Purpose 'I want to enjoy my time'. What physical action do you need to take to achieve that Purpose? None. There is nothing you *physically* have to 'do' to enjoy your time in this situation, you simply have the Purpose. This is an example of a *mental action* being all that is needed to achieve a Purpose. Another example is wanting to achieve the Purpose 'I want to be superior', let's say, while listening to a university lecture. Again, this Purpose is not achieved by saying or doing anything because one can feel superior to the lecturer while sitting still, without saying anything.

When you stroke a dog it is a physical action which you perform because you had the mental action of 'I care' or 'I enjoy' in the first place. The physical action of stroking comes from having these mental actions – or simply Actions – as we will refer to them from now on. If 'I want to be superior' is my Purpose during my university lecture, I will need to use the Action 'I condescend' to the lecturer. While I'm mentally condescending to the lecturer I will feel superior and my Purpose is achieved. While lying in the sun I have the Action 'I enjoy' or 'I revel' towards the feeling of heat. These Actions are the way I achieve my Purpose of 'I want to enjoy my time'.

The way we achieve *all* Purposes is through Actions, physical actions are the result of mental ones.

Although not overt, Actions are more important than gestures or words. Words are just words, whereas Actions are the truth behind the words. They are how we feel about the subject.

When someone says, 'I love you', it can mean many different things depending on the Action behind it. A couple have just had an argument, it's now over and resolved but one lover is feeling uncertain or insecure and the words "I love you" may come from the other with the Action 'I reassure'. In a different scenario, where a partner is controlling and wants to get their own way, they may say the same words with the Action 'I provoke guilt' – to manipulate the other. Let's say this argument didn't get resolved and it's now tense in the room...one of the lovers knows they are about to be dumped and the words "I love you" are said with the Action 'I plead'.

The words are the same (even the physical behaviour may seem the same) but the Action behind the words reveals the truth.

At some point in our very distant past, language as we know it didn't exist but humans still had to attack, love, warn, encourage, etc. For hundreds of thousands of years there were no words and Actions were the only way to communicate. Even now that we have words, Actions are still the way we *really* communicate. This is why when someone is unhappy, we know without them having to say so... We know that we can't trust someone even though they say we can... Or someone apologises and we know they don't mean it, no matter what is said.

Two people can behave the same way, say the same things and get different responses – it all depends on their Actions.

Two people tell the same joke, one with the Action 'I entertain' and the other (who doesn't like telling jokes) with the Action 'I doubt', 'I shrink' or even 'I humiliate myself'.

To reiterate, Actions are what we do to achieve our Purposes. Everything else is a manifestation of this. If 'I want to be secure', I'm likely to have the Action, 'I brace myself', which may result in my shoulders tensing and a change in my facial expression.

Actions are often the easiest element of invisible thinking to see. For instance, when someone, tells you something and you don't believe them, it's often their Action (e.g. 'I doubt' or 'I cover up') which gives them away. We notice people's Actions all the time but usually unawarely. Start to see if you can awarely identify them. Have you noticed when some inconsistency in a person's behaviour is pointed out to us *after* an incident, we will often recognise it (e.g. "Oh yes…my goodness that's right, she did seem uncomfortable") – but if it hadn't been pointed we wouldn't have seen it. This is what this book is about; understanding that you have this Awareness all the time and arriving at a place where you notice what is going on in each present moment. In the second section of the book we will show you how to train your brain to slow down enough to be able to watch your Awareness (moment by moment) whenever you want to.

Actions are the relationship between oneself and the object of attention (e.g. myself and the lecturer, myself and the sun) and are always expressed as 'I', followed by a verb. For example, 'I regret', 'I guide', I demand obedience', 'I encourage', 'I pity myself', 'I gloat', 'I panic', 'I lose myself', 'I long for', 'I dread'… You'll see many more in Appendix Two.

Actions have a direction in space and it's interesting to see how this works. Imagine you are chatting with a friend in a coffee shop, but you are thinking about having left the cooker gas lit after having made your eggs this morning. You carry on the conversation with the person in front of you and yet your mind keeps going to your kitchen, or by now, possibly to your apartment being on fire. Because your Actions are directed to a different space than where you are, the conversation with your friend might be unclear.

Actions also have a direction in time. In anticipating your next meal, your Action is directed towards the future. If you are reflecting on an argument you had yesterday when you told off your partner, and now with hindsight you realise you were in the wrong, your (possible) Action, 'I regret' is being directed towards the past.

Actions have varying degrees of strength as well. Think about the Action you're using while reading this book. It's probably a gentle 'I contemplate', 'I consider' or 'I find out'. Now imagine reading some important information you've been given just before a court case. The kind of Action would be the same or similar, but the *intensity* of the Action would be greater. The intensity of an Action, in its varying degrees, can alter the name of an Action. The Actions 'I brush off', 'I reject', 'I stand my ground', 'I defend myself' and 'I attack'… are all different degrees of the same Action. Likewise, 'I shrink', 'I retreat' and 'I run away'. The strength of an Action tells you a lot about the strength of feeling behind it.

In everyday life, we can have a number of Actions in any given period of time. Referring to the shortest time period, these are called Basic Actions. If you've just been told you can't do something, you might have a Basic Action 'I regret', but then straight away you think of an alternative, this comes with 'I enjoy'. Notice how quickly Basic Actions change.

Actions which last for longer periods are called Main Actions. Main Actions exist to achieve our medium-term Purposes. For instance, if you're talking to your bank manager about getting a loan, your Main Action throughout the meeting might be 'I do my best'.

This Main Action will be held for as long as you have the same Purpose and will change when your Purpose does. For the duration of the interview you would have one Main Action, 'I do my best' but there would be many Basic Actions; in one moment you may 'impress' and in another, 'ingratiate', but always in the context of the Main Action – 'I do my best'.

Action
What I do to achieve my Purpose

Devices

When they were students, John and Harry knew each other well but they haven't seen each other for years. By chance they bump into each other at a seminar and spend some time together. At the end of the seminar they are about to part company when Harry says, "We should catch up again sometime", to which John replies, "Yeah, sure!".

Sound familiar?

Although John said, "Yeah, sure!", he already has an impression that he and Harry have exhausted their conversation and no longer share much in common. So, although John agreed to meet up with Harry again, he knew he wasn't going to. He said, "Yes" where he meant "No" (a fascinating human trait that animals are well free of).

Like John, you will have at some time said one thing but thought something else. Then, like John, you will have used a Device.

Devices are used to cover up our Actions. John's Action was really 'I reject' but he covered it up with the Device, 'I look forward'.

We use Devices because we want people to think that we have different thoughts to those which we have; often because of social etiquette, to ingratiate ourselves, to avoid upsetting people or to manipulate a situation.

If an Action is what I think, then a Device is what I want people to think I think. First dates and interviews hold a minefield of examples of this. Devices are often used to create (manipulate) first impressions.

Where Actions have varying strengths, Devices have varying *transparencies* which affect how well one can see through them. In the example above, John used a Device to avoid an uncomfortable moment but also because he didn't want Harry to get in touch again. John made his Device opaque enough so that Harry didn't feel too uncomfortable, but transparent enough for there to be adequate doubt in Harry's mind to put him off contacting John in the future. John definitely didn't strategise this thinking; his mind would have automatically done it for him in the given circumstances.

Devices
What I want others to think I do

This chapter gives new meaning to the phrase "Actions speak louder than words".

EXERCISE 6

Shop assistants or waiters can be helpful for this exercise as they often give unusual, unexpected or unhelpful responses to simple transactions (it gets more interesting if you complain or return an item – but you don't have to do that for this exercise).

The next few times you go shopping or eat out, make a point of thinking about the response you get from the people serving you. Don't do or say anything different, just allow the impression of the way they spoke to you to sit in your mind and see if you can find out their Actions – e.g. 'I tell off' ('I was about to go on my break'), 'I ingratiate myself' ('My boss is watching me on the security camera), 'I preen' ('Hello!'). You can use the list of Actions in Appendix Two to help. It will take time at first but you'll get the hang of it.

Keep an eye on your own Actions and Purposes throughout this exercise, as these can come into play and affect your perspective while you are watching others.

This chapter is also the last of the seven chapters of Part One which have discussed *Why We Think the Way We Do*. These chapters will very likely have excavated many thoughts that you hadn't considered before, enabling you to see much more of the unaware thinking that you've had throughout your life. This means that since starting this book you have a greater Awareness of what you think, why you think it and are becoming clearer on the thoughts you want to be free of.

Or conversely, perhaps what you have read so far has brought up things that you don't want to think about?

Or maybe it simply all seems too much?

Well, don't lose heart!

You're in the right place.

Everything that has come up needed to surface for you to deal with it. You needed to see what was there, what was *really* there, before we could launch into Part Two.

But before we do, let's remind ourselves of why you are now in a much better position to make changes to your life (your health, relationships, career, sex-life…) by having a quick recap on what we've covered.

Initially, we looked at Mind Erosions; how we create them and how – because we are so deep in our ditches – we do not even know that we have them. This led us to the important (because this whole book rests on it) subject of developing and expanding our Awareness – developing the ability to see more of our thinking.

Awareness is the key to seeing previously unaware Mind Erosions. And in turn, what catalyses the expansion of our Awareness, are our EAs – our earliest memories and our thoughts behind them. The same thoughts, as we went on to see, that formed a dictatorial role in the running of our lives.

Next came a discussion about Complexes; thoughts that are connected to other thoughts. By understanding how Complexes work we can see how strongly Complexes contribute to us being drawn into repeating patterns of thinking/behaviour… over and over again… regardless of whether they hinder or support the direction we want our lives to go in.

The Events chapter introduced the concept of intensified thinking (as opposed to Happenings); the concentrated thinking we have about an aspect of our lives that we perceive to be true, whether it really is or not. This thinking influences our lives long after an original Happening has passed because we take our interpretation of what originally took place into new Happenings. In the long term, this means that we are repeatedly recreating old experiences. This (as with all aspects of the Mind Erosion) is a great hindrance to being able to approach each new Happening in our lives with fresh eyes, open to new outcomes and greater possibilities.

Purposes brought the subject of 'happiness' to the fore, and how everything we do, we do because we think it will make us happy. HOWEVER! it may have been alarming to find out that our ideas of happiness have often been greatly affected by dysfunctional experiences in our early life. We saw how Purposes are usually invisible to us and how they contradict our visible intentions, creating confusion, suffering and stalling our ability to get on with our lives. This chapter will have directed you to take a much closer and more honest look at what your Purposes really are.

The topic of Actions covered what we do to achieve our Purposes and how useful it is to be aware of our Actions. Actions give us good insight into the Purposes we are *really* using and they explain how we use Devices to disguise what we are genuinely thinking.

Mindprint covered the main elements of our important, generalised, invisible thoughts. Just as a fingerprint is unique to an individual, so too is their Mindprint – no two people have the same Mindprint. We went through the different components, all described as Events to emphasise that the Mindprint is comprised of 'intensified thinking' (about different aspects of life) and not a reflection of reality.

Having a good look at your Mindprint and discovering the elements that are at work for you will give you many areas to explore when you decide to revisit the previous chapters. You will be able to go deeper into how the different subjects pertain specifically to you... Doing this will also be a useful reference as we move into Part Two.

The Formation of Consciousness chapter focused on how most of the conditioned thinking that plays a large part in our everyday life (and has been surfacing as you read this book), initially came into existence. We looked at how our thinking was especially conditioned by the relationships we had with the people who looked after us and the resulting Cogs. We looked at how, as children, we were put in situations that we didn't know how to understand or how to respond to. And how, subsequently, this lead to much of the UT and shame affecting our lives today.

Part One of this book serves to bring a lot of what were previously unaware thoughts to your aware mind, for you to see the different components and mechanics of your mind and to see how these different elements have made you the way you are.

The first eight chapters identified aspects of your thinking that you may like to change, thoughts that are not working in your best interest and are keeping you in ditches that you are ready to climb out of.

Part One gave you the information to understand *Why We Think The Way We Do* and having arrived here, you are now more than ready for Part Two where we are going to look at *How To Change It*.

PART 2
AND HOW TO CHANGE IT

Chapter Eight
Finishing-off Thinking

We have extensively covered the thinking that comprises our Consciousness and how it affects our lives. Now we are going to see what can be done about it.

If you have read the chapters consecutively, you will be familiar with the term 'Unfinished Thinking' and have an impression of what this means. You will also be aware of Shame Events, how they are formed and how Shame Events are at the bottom of most, if not all, Unfinished Thinking.

Unfinished Thinking, and the Shame Events that cause them, are the major reason why you might feel something is wrong with your life. They cause confusion because they invisibly stop you doing what you visibly want to. Moreover, Shame Events make you fail because you contort your life for the shame to remain undiscovered. All of this stunts your personal development, stalls your career prospects, ruins your relationships and (if all this isn't enough) Unfinished Thinking and Shame Events will spoil your joy of life itself. This background noise sits in your mind, causing you on-going suffering.

The above isn't written to shock you (well, maybe a little) but it is to emphasise the debilitating affect that shame and Unfinished Thinking have on our lives.

Generally, people look towards, and blame outside of themselves for the cause of their problems (family, friends, employers, politicians etc.), whereas it's our own thinking that that is the source of it all.

Sometimes we sense or know this, so why do we never look at this thinking?

Because at the root of all Unfinished Thinking and shame is fear.

The following example will explain.

Lucy goes up to her mother and says, "Mummy, can I...?" but before she gets any further with her question, her mother cuts in, "Oh, not now Lucy. Can't you see I'm busy?". This wasn't a big Event and Lucy didn't feel as though she had been told off, but she did notice that her mother didn't look busy as she was just reading the newspaper. The first time this happened Lucy orientated and wondered, 'Why is Mum saying this?'

A little later the same week, Lucy again asks her mother a question, who again 'doesn't have time for her' and again Lucy can't understand her mother's response. On the third occasion, Lucy's impression has changed from orientating herself to having a feeling that something is wrong. It isn't long before unpleasant thoughts start to flash across Lucy's mind such as, "My mother doesn't love me...', 'My mother doesn't care...', 'I'm not loved...' or 'I'm unworthy...'

Simultaneously in these moments, she feels fear.

Fear, because having these thoughts as a child is very frightening, close to overwhelming.

Lucy's mother never explains herself, nor does little Lucy know how to understand her mother's dismissive reaction. All that Lucy comes away with is a stuck thought that if her own mother, the one who should love and care for her the most, is not interested in answering her questions then how can she (Lucy) be of any value to her? Lucy's train of thought continues with: 'If I am rejected by my very own mother then I must be worthless...' and here Lucy's 'thinking it through' abruptly ends.

Does this reaction sound over the top?

Consider that these are not the thoughts of a grown-up who has seen it all before, but of a child. Children are inherently vulnerable and sensitive; reflect on how easily a child can get upset, cry or be terrified.

Lucy, as a young child, knows nothing of the (big wide) world, and most of what she does know she has relied on her parents to explain. Consider too, that if you or I had a similar Event today it would be one of many Events in our (longer) lifetimes and therefore, not so significant. In comparison, a child has had a fractional number of experiences where each one is potentially very significant. Do not underestimate how powerful an Event like Lucy had with her mother can be to a child, and how it was to you!

Liken the situation to a smooth flat tablet of soft clay. As we grow up every Event we have marks this tablet. By the time we are adults, there are so many marks from the many Events of our life that any new one will have to be big and deep to stand out. A child's tablet, in comparison, has hardly any marks, so each Event stands out as important, if not formative.

Taking this metaphor together with Lucy's vulnerability of knowing that she needs her mother to support her and to show her how to live, she has fear. The fear is rooted in thinking that, 'If I am so unworthy of my mother's love and care, what value have I compared to others and therefore, what kind of life will I grow up to have?' and 'With Mum treating me like this, how will I ever be able to know how to live…? What will become of me?'

The implications of these thoughts are so frightening that Lucy (alas, like all of us) decides not to think them in the slightest, instead choosing to lose herself by thinking/doing something else… Leaving the thought 'Unfinished'.

Although! when you lose yourself from a thought, it doesn't disappear – it stays in your head. It starts as a Ghoul, a little frightening thought, which when joined by other Ghouls – because of many similar Events – it grows and becomes a Ghost (see Mindprint), seriously affecting your life.

When adult Lucy was asked about the consequence of these experiences on her adult life, she saw that there were many:

Firstly, because of the frequent repetition of these thoughts throughout her childhood, Lucy acquired a deep Mind Erosion. She often found herself thinking thoughts associated with these scenarios, even when they were out of context of her present situation.

Secondly, adult Lucy noticed that she had created a Complex of 'abruptly ending thoughts when they are interrupted by fear', rather than thinking thoughts through to their conclusion. In other words, Lucy found she had created a Mind Erosion of creating Unfinished Thinking. This means that when Lucy experiences something that bothers her, her tendency (and this is true of all of us) is to 'lose herself' from it rather than think it through... Creating even more Unfinished Thinking.

Thirdly, Lucy saw that her Unfinished Thinking created new and equally destructive thoughts. Chapters Five and Six (The Formation of Consciousness and Mindprint chapters) discuss how our thoughts about men and women (and ourselves) are shaped by our male and female PiCs. Because of the Events with her mother and variations on it with her father, Lucy acquired the thought, 'My mother/father doesn't love me'. In her adult life, this translated into the thought: 'Men/women are superior' and/or the Ghost: 'I can't be loved'. This led to a variety of problems in all her relationships. As we've said before, if we have an important thought we will actively try to prove it is true.

Fourthly, the outcome of Lucy growing up with thoughts like 'My mother doesn't love me' or 'I am worthless or unlovable' is that, although mostly invisible, these thoughts take up a large proportion of her thinking capacity; making it hard for her to concentrate on even mundane matters. These thoughts also prevent her from thinking clearly and, evidently, they obstruct her living a happy and fulfilled life.

Do you recognise any of Lucy's story, patterns or tendencies in yourself?

Remember – it's OK if you do, AND...you know what...however *real* it feels, *it's all only thinking* and thinking can be changed.

The nature of invisible thinking is precisely that, invisible, and if invisible thinking is the stuff that is really running our lives, what is its relationship to our visible thinking?

We have stated that Unfinished Thinking is based on shame and because of this we want to hide it from others. This, makes us fail, which we would rather do, and lie to ourselves that we are doing it, than go to the (granted, uncomfortable) root of our shame and face it square on. We continue to *visibly* think that we want to have a fulfilled life and are free to pursue all avenues and possibilities but *invisibly* this is not the case at all; we are failing and lying to ourselves and others to cover it up. Notice how the above demonstrates visible thinking being contradictory to our invisible thinking.

A good illustration of how visible thinking contradicts our invisible thinking is what took place when adult Lucy decided to apply for a new job. Lucy interviewed for several jobs over a period of three weeks. All were jobs that she was more than adequately qualified for. Lucy worked hard at preparing for the interviews and thought to herself, 'I am going to show them why I am the best person for the job'.

But Lucy didn't get any offers from them, no second interviews, no positive feedback, nothing. Lucy couldn't understand why. Lucy subsequently spent another two years in a job she didn't like and was overqualified for.

Later, with more Awareness, Lucy reflected on her preparation for those interviews. At first, she simply remembered working hard on the preparation but going deeper she remembered being bothered by the amount of work she was doing. Even though she was very qualified, Lucy remembered an impression of stress. As she probed this impression, she realised the stress was because she felt that no matter how hard she worked, the interviewers (like her parents) weren't going to be interested in her. Lucy realised that throughout her intense preparation, she had been thinking that 'No one is going to listen to me anyway'.

This lack of confidence came from Lucy's Shame Event, 'I'm worthless'. Her EA set a precedent that was repeating itself throughout her life and again, now in her interviews. This thinking affected all her preparation, the answers she gave in the interviews, and especially the Purpose she used when she gave those answers, 'I want to be rejected'. The interviewers did not notice any of these specifics, they only felt that she was not what they were looking for.

Can you see how *visibly* Lucy thought, 'I am the best person for the job and this is why...', but *invisibly* she thought, 'Why would anyone want to give me a job'. See how her visible thinking contradicts her invisible thinking?

Can you also see the extent to which the Unfinished Thinking, born in Lucy's childhood, distorted her adult life? Rather than thinking I am who 'I' am, 'I' has become someone who is 'worthless'. Believing that she is worthless became Lucy's point of reference and the more this Complex strengthened, the more Lucy's world became based on her Unfinished Thinking rather than her present circumstances.

It must be repeated that Lucy's thinking was not visible to her at the time. She could only see it once she had learned to explore her Unfinished Thinking. It must also be added that Lucy isn't unique in thinking such debilitating thoughts – we all have thoughts like this.

Unfinished Thinking distorts our view of reality, making it harder to think clearly and interact with the world as it is. It causes us to warp reality so that *the world fits to what we think.* Increasingly, this leads to conflict when interacting with the 'outside world', which can feel anything from pointless to confusing, lonely or painful...right through to anguished and fractured!

> *"A man's life is what his thoughts make of it."*
> *Roman philosopher, Marcus Aurelius[6]*

Being aware of what Marcus Aurelius is pointing out here, is one of the biggest steps to an increasingly free and 'real' reality.

When we are children, thoughts like those Lucy was trying to process in relation to her mother and herself are hard to comprehend or know what to do with. As adults, we understand life better, especially when we decide to look at our thinking, revisit our memories and deal with the ones we once couldn't.

Finishing-off Thinking means going back to the initial formation of our thoughts and thinking through what – at the time – we were unable (or in later life, unwilling) to do.

Finishing-off Thinking
Taking thoughts beyond the point where they were interrupted by fear

'Finishing-off Thinking' is quite a mouthful, so from here on we'll use the abbreviation, FoffTing.

It may be helpful to visualise every Unfinished Thought as a coiled up brass clock spring. FoffTing is the untangling or straightening out of one such brass spring by placing one forefinger on one end of the coil and using (from all the guidance in this book) your other hand to slowly unroll the coil and straighten it out.

Figure 8.1 Clock spring – Unfinished Thinking

Uncoiling a coil sure sounds easy but it's an ongoing process rather than something that is immediately achieved. Like a brass spring, unless Unfinished Thinking is given sufficient time and attention to keep it straightened, when you take away your finger – that's your attention – it will roll back up. Though not always as tightly as it was at the start. If this happens, simply unroll it again. Then, if/when you take your finger off and it rolls up again, the coil will be looser, more uncoiled than ever before…and you carry on this process until the wire is uncoiled and remains uncoiled long after you have taken away your finger.

Figure 8.2 Uncoiling the spring

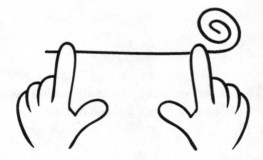

Figure 8.3 Uncoiled spring

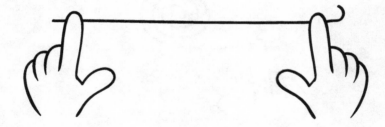

FoffTing is fundamental to increasing your Awareness and to eliminating the (unfortunately) many fears that were rooted in childhood. In turn, your Unfinished Thinking is replaced by the space and freedom for an easier, more enjoyable and substantially more fulfilled life.

The Purpose of this chapter is to provide you with the direction and guidance to identify your Unfinished Thoughts and to help you finish them off.

***

FoffTing may seem a daunting process, but be assured that you have already started and are well on your way without even realising it (is that relief?). As we repeatedly acknowledge – from the start of this book, memories have surfaced and your attention will have been directed to impressions you have about your life that perhaps you hadn't seen before, or maybe an old thought has been nagging at you. These are ways that FoffTing begins; by looking at a memory or impression or a pattern of thinking/behaviour and then thinking it through. EAs in the Awareness or Mindprint chapters may have triggered your memories...as will have some of the other examples in the book (a cunning ploy on the part of the writers). It may be obvious but worth pointing out; the older the memory (that is, the younger you were when the memory took place), the longer you have invisibly been thinking that thought... therefore, the longer it has been influencing your thoughts. So, if EAs are already popping up, you are in a good place to start.

Together with memories surfacing from childhood, another way to start FoffTing is to look at your state of mind now, at this very moment. Often, we have a feeling that something is bothering us right now but we usually abandon the thought by losing ourselves from it, whereas this is the ideal opportunity to find out what we *really* think.

Jim is a decorator and on the day in question, whilst painting a door, he feels relaxed and content. A little time has passed and he is now close to finishing the door when he notices his mood change, and rather than feeling at peace he now feels depressed. Something is making him feel heavy and uneasy but he doesn't know what or why.

In the past, Jim would have considered this 'his mood' and left it at that, but because he has been taught some of the tools in this book he takes this opportunity to think about what has just taken place.

Jim wants to know what he was thinking that caused his change in mood and where the thought originated from. Jim decides to trace back the chain of thoughts he's had over the last 10 to 20 minutes; working backwards from the time when he noticed he was suffering back to when he was feeling content. Doing this, Jim reaches a thought he had been thinking about his father – that he hadn't spoken to his Dad in a while – and Jim saw that guilt was the key to triggering his mood change. Returning to this thought and giving himself time to look at it, Jim saw that this thought was just a thought, and yet he had suffered with it because it was part of a Complex connected to suffering.

Jim recognised that normally this Complex would have been *unawarely* activated and that by now *awarely* seeing it, the suffering instantly subsided. In this way (seeing one's thinking, increasing ones Awareness), one can improve their life every day. Why suffer when you don't need to?!

Jim could have left this here as this simple approach had already made his day, but Jim knew the suffering he had was obviously connected to other parts of his Mindprint (no such thing as a loose thought) to do with his father. Contemplating this further and by asking himself additional questions, Jim made greater inroads to the roots of his thinking. Jim realised that he had a pattern of not calling his father which always left him feeling guilty; in this he saw he had the Purpose, 'I want to feel guilty'. The point we're honing in on is that even with very little investigation, Jim had started the uncoiling process. You see – you don't have to wait for a major catastrophe or problem to surface in your life to start looking at the thinking you have. You can start now, at this very moment, and get the process started.

Visible Thought Analysis

Visible Thought Analysis (VTA) is the analysis of the wider Complex of thoughts that are attached to everyday visible thoughts. VTA comprises a visible thought and the (unaware) Purposes and Mindprint elements.

To start with you need a visible thought. Visible thoughts, if you remember from Chapter One, are those which you are aware of as you go through life, like 'I'm hungry', 'Oh shit! I'm going to be late', 'That girl/boy is gorgeous', 'Get off my foot, you asshole', etc.

Next, simply catch yourself thinking something, anything, and write it down. You might be buying a shirt and think, 'No, it's too small', or you're on the bus and some rowdy people get on and you think, 'I'll get off at this stop', or you're having a productive day and think, 'It's going really well'. These thoughts might seem innocuous but the invisible thoughts behind them often aren't.

A VTA consists of six components and the first three are Purposes. Remember that we are always looking to satisfy Purposes. We start the VTA by identifying the 1) Short-term Purpose, 2) Medium-term Purpose and 3) Long-term Purpose attached to the visible thought we are looking at (we've not come across short-term Purposes before. They are, as the name implies, Purposes that are achieved very quickly).

After this has been done, we look for the next three VTA components; these are the Mindprint Events: 4) Self Event, 5) People Event and 6) Life Event attached to the visible thought we are working with. These are the thoughts about yourself, people and life that influenced this thought.

This isn't hard work, nor should it be intimidating. If you are ready to get to know yourself, this is a captivating process of self-understanding where what you find can be very insightful.

Here's an example:

William walks out of his house on his way to work and sees that his car is dirty. His visible thought is 'I must wash the car'. Further down the road, William wonders if such a mundane thought could have any Unfinished Thinking attached to it. As William reflects on 'I must wash the car' he sees impressions of having a hard life and of wanting no responsibilities. So, while his visible thought looks positive (getting the car clean) the invisible looks less so (it surfaced his less-than-pleasant thoughts about life).

This is how the VTA worked out:

1. **Short-term Purpose:** *'I want to lose myself'*
    ...from having to wash the car.
    Because William knew he wasn't going to wash his car anytime soon.

2. **Medium-term Purpose:** *'I want to have a peaceful life'*
    ...with as few nagging/troubling thoughts as possible.

Note how the Short-term Purpose helps William achieve his medium-term Purpose.

3. **Long-term Purpose:** *'Happiness is always failing'*
   In wanting to have a peaceful life (his Medium-term Purpose), William often rejected opportunities because he thought they would conflict with his idea of a peaceful life. But! because he knew this also meant he was missing out on life opportunities (new experiences), his mind understood this to be failing. Thus, over time, the Purpose of 'wanting to fail' developed.

4. **Self Event:** *'I'm a failure'*
   Successful people have other people wash their cars for them. It isn't that William thinks that having to wash his car makes him a failure, it's that he already thinks he's a failure, and having to wash his own car is confirmation of this.

5. **People Event:** *'People are judgemental'*
   William only thought to clean his car because of what others would think.

6. **Life Event:** *'Life is hard'*
   The context for this thought can be summarised by 'I have to struggle to appear to still be in the game (of life) when really I know I've given up'.

This simple analysis illustrates that although the visible thought, 'I must wash my car' seems mundane, the thoughts behind it reveal much more.

With your first VTA you'll probably find the six components are vague; lacking in any 'meat' or details. If this is the case and your answers leave you feeling nothing, then you need to do some more digging. Give yourself the time to do this, there is no rush, it's always worth it and remember to be honest with yourself.

The very nature of Complexes – that there is no such thing as a loose thought – indicates that any thought will lead you to other thoughts. By using the VTA as a guide, you have a route to finding invisible thoughts that you wouldn't otherwise know were there (affecting your moods, choices…your life).

Something that can help identify the invisible thoughts beneath the visible is to ask yourself what would be the funniest, cringiest or most anger-provoking thought you could have that you don't want to see i.e. look for what bothers you or would bother you the most to think was true. Your final answer is likely to 'hit a nerve' or 'press a button' or make you laugh (with recognition) – that's when you know you're on the right track. William, for instance, noticed a combination of humour and wincing when he identified 'Life is Hard' as his Life Event in the VTA. This reaction indicated that he'd hit bull's eye, otherwise it wouldn't have bothered him.

We all make judgements about the thinking/behaviour of others; things that we don't think are right or which we disapprove of. But be sure to notice when you cringe or get angry or laugh (dismissively or nervously) or any other unusual reaction... at the suggestion that you have this thinking yourself, because this is a good indication that you think these very thoughts. You may have had some of these reactions when you read the list of Purposes in Appendix One.

Stages of FoffTing

Working through a VTA, considering an EA, or simply reading the examples in this book will reveal thoughts that range from those you would prefer not to have to those grossly affecting your life. With this as a starting point, there are certain stages or steps to go through to Finish-off this thinking. These stages don't come in any strict order and the stages will certainly overlap and get revisited as you work with your Unfinished Thinking. The order of the next sections is the closest to a sequence for you to follow.

1. Going Limp

What should you do when you see you have Unfinished Thinking or some deeply embedded thought(s) influencing or even controlling your life?

What should you do with these thoughts?

Nothing.

Eh?

Yes, that's right.
Nothing.
Stay with us and this will become clearer.

It may seem bewildering at first, but doing nothing is crucial, and often sufficient, to loosening the strength of thoughts/Complexes. By doing nothing, a disconnecting, letting go or melting away takes place in the relationship between one's mind and the thought(s) in question. It's akin to weakening the neural circuit that activated the thought and the activated thought itself.

By doing nothing what we mean is, to 'Go Limp'.

Go Limp
To physically and mentally relax on a thought(s)

By Going Limp, the mind says, 'This (Unfinished Thinking) isn't important to me' or 'I don't need this', instead of rejecting it or judging the thought as '*bad*'. This doesn't mean ignoring the thought (and definitely not losing yourself from it) but allowing it to be there, and watching it in action. When we Go Limp we are neutrally disabling a thought.

Anything other than Going Limp sustains and/or strengthens your relationship with the thought. If you punish your thoughts, this Affinity is added to the Complex and the focus becomes *punishing* the thought rather than letting it go. Similarly, if you condescend to your thoughts (e.g. 'Oh that's the thought I picked up from my mother'; accompanied by you rolling your eyes), *that* Affinity is added, and you are, again, strengthening the Mind Erosion rather than weakening the thought…and so on. Unless you Go Limp, you are always adding more inputs to the Complex instead of Finishing it off.

You likely may not have noticed but you will always have had certain Actions attached to your Unfinished thoughts, such as 'I revel', 'I wallow', 'I suffer' or 'I sulk'; but having become so used to these Actions, you no longer notice them. To truly allow these thoughts to dissolve you must Go Limp.

Once you've identified some Unfinished Thinking not only is Going Limp the most effective tool you have in dealing with it, it is also your Emergency First Response. Going Limp is so critical to FoffTing that much of this chapter is dedicated to explaining what it is and how to do it.

Going Limp is a mental impression that we all naturally have but recognising it amongst all the other impressions in our mind can take some consideration. To help you create an impression of what Going Limp is, imagine yourself in each of the scenarios below. The scenarios are not examples of what you need to do to Go Limp; they, individually and collectively illustrate the impression of what Going Limp is:

- Imagine a river which, although beautiful to look at, has some ugly debris slowly floating down it. So, before you can enjoy the view, you have to patiently wait for the debris to pass. There is no need (and no point) in getting stressed, frustrated or annoyed; simply calmly allow the current to move the debris in its own time so you can enjoy the view.

- You are lying on the ground and around you are nondescript shapes kicking you, not in a way that it's painful, but enough that it is difficult to tolerate – and you do nothing. All you do is wait and see what is going to happen while lying still and without putting up any resistance whatsoever.

- You are at a party and around you there are people talking and dancing. People are laughing, telling stories and some may even mention your name. You let it all this happen without reacting to any of it; you completely let go of the outside world.

- You are lying down, face up while relaxing on a floating air mattress in the middle of a lake, your feet and hands are gently dangling in the water. Around you are buoys and even though they gently bump into you, you do not react; you may feel the temptation to touch, push or grab onto them but you just simply allow them to be there, gently bumping into you without reacting.

Going Limp is a relaxing sensation – the feeling of completely letting go of any inputs to your senses and surrendering your stresses.

Here are some examples of Going Limp from people lives:

Alan is walking to college one day when he becomes aware of a mental impression that he recognises he has almost every day. Alan notices that he has a feeling of apprehension or even fear of what the day will bring. Alan decides to Finish-off this fear by simply bringing to mind the impression of Going Limp…and within a few moments the feeling subsides. The next day Alan notices the fear again and so he repeats Going Limp…but this time the feeling doesn't go away. Alan feels that the first time he did this he had 'caught the thinking off guard' and his Going Limp was successful but for some reason it wasn't working this time. Realising this was probably some kind of invisible self sabotage getting in the way. Alan repeats Going Limp each morning for the next few days and sees that each day it gets easier to let this feeling of fear dissipate away.

Remember that thoughts are just thoughts, they are not real, they are just chemicals and electricity in our minds – *we do not need to have one thought any more than another.* What may seem like very strong or very important thoughts, like those to do with personal relationships, are still just thoughts.

Chloe's relationship with her family, like that of many people, has its problems. Chloe often visits her parents and finds that when she leaves she regrets that she's had the same conversation with them that they always have. She leaves with a feeling of sulking towards her parents because they won't change, as well as despair for herself that nothing can be done. In advance of one visit, however, Chloe decides to Go Limp to see what will happen. The day before, Chloe prepares her state of mind (this will be explained later) so that she can Go Limp no matter what happens or how she feels. The result of this new approach is that (for the very first time) Chloe sees her parents as people in their own right, and not the generalised impression of 'parents' who she has wished were different. Being able to see them as people, just like everyone else, is the starting point for her being able to Finish-off her sulk with them.

Bronwyn's family have a history of mental illness and, as a consequence, she has always had a fear that she has elements (however minor) of 'mad' thinking. This fearful thought sits in her mind and has created behaviour that is very stressful: Bronwyn always feels she must be extra prepared at work in case she is asked something and her answer gives away her 'mental state'. She puts in extra hours in case her 'faulty mind' affects her work within the nine-to-five day and she always feels she must find new ways to show her dedication in case her boss decides to fire someone – and if people find out that she is 'mad' she'll be the first to go.

This thinking and its consequences make Bronwyn's life exhausting and close to unbearable. She realises that if she doesn't do anything about the situation, she will indeed go mad from the stress alone! So, one Friday, Bronwyn leaves work thinking, 'That's it, I can't live like this anymore' and, over the weekend, Bronwyn prepares her mind (as will be explained in section 3) to completely Go Limp on Monday morning, simply to see what happens. Bronwyn decides, that if she is going to completely 'fuck everything up', as her fear had led her to believe, and everyone is to see that 'something is wrong with her', well so be it. At least she'll be free from the stress of holding on to all these thoughts.

Monday comes and the morning passes and... her day is stress free, she gets more work done, makes fewer mistakes and (as she found out later) her colleagues remark to each other how much easier she is to work with. The 'highly strung' element to her personality has gone. It was after all only the thought – her fear that she is mad – that was fuelling her problems and, as we have seen, her mental pictures meant she had the Purpose to be seen to be mad.

Monday (with Bronwyn's new resolve) served as a point of reference for how life could be and, in time, she removed more of the extraneous stresses that had dogged her. By Going Limp, Bronwyn had made space in her head to be the normal woman she was.

Going Limp is important to FoffTing because our Unfinished Thinking has never been dealt with in this way before. From the moment the thought was created, however many years ago, we immediately repressed it and left it that way ever since. By repressing the thought, we made it Important, and this kept it alive. By Going Limp, you allow the thought to dissipate as it should have done when it was created and, in so doing, the thought simply becomes a circumstance of your past.

Generally, Going Limp is done once some Unfinished Thinking has been recognised.

Here's another example: Bradley is a student who for seemingly no reason provokes his teachers' (any teacher's) anger when in class. Bradley does this by continuously asking the teacher awkward and unnecessary questions. After this pattern is pointed out, Bradley remembers a related EA.

As a child, Bradley spends most of his time with his mother. The rare occasions that he and his father go out together are very important and, like all little boys, he enjoys belonging with his Dad. In one memory however, Bradley did something which led to his father slapping him. This EA left him with two impressions – one of his father's anger and the other of belonging with his father. These two impressions merged to form a Complex between abuse and belonging which created the guideline, 'Abused people are loved/belong'.

Remember, that whatever happens to us in our childhood, be it care or abuse, it is *always* perceived as security. And, however bizarre it may seem (and we all have bizarre elements to our thinking), this was why adult Bradley would often provoke people's anger, especially with PiCs, as this gives him a feeling of security. Bradley isn't necessarily after an actual slap but something like a telling-off or disciplinary action will suffice. Even to be told to "Fuck off!" by his friends is close enough to the comfort of that early memory of belonging with his Dad – which had become more important to him than anything (remember the UC).

What can Bradley do to Finish-off the thought 'Abused people are loved/belong'?

Firstly, the pattern must become clear to Bradley. The thought has to be put into the right words to nail it, rather than, 'I just feel like challenging the teacher (or friends, family etc) and I don't know why'. Bradley needs to see how his pattern keeps recurring.

Once Bradley has identified the thought and sees how it works in his life, he needs to decide that whenever he sees his 'I want to provoke anger' surfacing, he should bring in the impression of Going Limp, and let it fill his mind.

That's all.

See the thought and let it be there.

It's important that Bradley doesn't try to 'stop' himself from provoking anger as this is repression. Instead, he needs to Go Limp and let whatever happens happen. The consequences are irrelevant. Chances are (as it was a very strong Complex) that, for a short while, Bradley will continue to provoke anger to some degree but each time it will be weaker as the Complex gets weaker.

Going Limp means that there is a way out, and you don't have to despair when you see you are in a Mind Erosion ditch. You can use Going Limp when it feels that there is nothing else you can do. If the thinking catches you unawares, or when the impression of it feels so strong or heavy or entrenched that you think there is no way out, you can always call on this Emergency First Response.

There may be times when you don't know what your precise Unfinished Thinking is but you have an unpleasant impression or sensation. Here, Go Limp, as it will still be effective, and by Going Limp you will gain the mental space to identify what the thought might be.

If Bradley continues to Go Limp, he will make his life a lot easier, although chances are his thinking will not shift permanently. Going Limp is incredibly effective by itself and to ensure a lasting effect it needs to be used alongside other FoffTing tools.

2. Watching Our Thinking – *'Seeing is Undoing'*

To Finish-off Unfinished Thinking properly, we need to know precisely what's there. Remember, thoughts do not lie in isolation; they're all connected to other thoughts and the more thoughts they are connected to, the stronger they are. This is like a bird's nest's strength, which is not derived from being made of twigs but from the number of twigs and how they are connected to many more. The more connections or inputs a Complex has the stronger it is.

To Finish-off a thought, we need to find out what the Complex is made up of. Equate it to a jigsaw puzzle which is easily recognisable when you see the whole picture but if you are only looking at one piece of the puzzle it is difficult to know what you are looking at. By only looking at a small part of a Complex it's difficult to understand the totality and so finish it off.

Returning to this book's principal subject of Awareness and the importance of seeing your thinking and keeping it visible: *the* key is to ask questions. Throughout the next section, you will see there are several ways to Finish-off your thoughts, but know that the essence of what you are doing is asking your mind to reveal your thoughts to you – and to do this you will be asking questions.

FoffTing is, in essence, asking questions. Asking questions sounds simple, and it is, but at first you may find it difficult to follow on from your initial question, because you do not have a Mind Erosion of doing this yet. The process will definitely become easier the more experience you have of (create a Complex of doing) it and, as with everything you do for the first time, you have to start somewhere. With a little practice and perseverance, the answers will come.

Go through your daily life as normal but keep the Purpose 'I want to find out' in your visible mind and see what comes up to help. It's best not to plan to do this at a particular time of day, such as 'in the evening', as the mind is skilled at preparing you to lose yourself when the allocated time comes. Make it something you do here and there when you have a few free moments, like when you're travelling, doing the dishes, making some coffee, during breaks at work, etc. Then, if you find yourself still thinking about it in the evening, fine. The point is to make it a regular thing.

Joseph is a man who for most of his life was reasonably fit and healthy, apart from a little asthma. As he approaches his forties, he notices that certain words trigger a reaction in him. At first it's a feeling that something is bothering him. Watching his thinking, he notices this reaction is to specific words like heart, cardiac, chest etc., which makes his thinking speed up with an impression of panic surfacing. Joseph knows about FoffTing and he quickly realises he has some Unfinished Thinking regarding his heart. Asking more questions, Joseph finds a memory (from age nine or ten) that he has of his mother telling him that his cousin had recently died of an "asthma-induced heart attack", as his mother had put it.

Up to that age, Joseph thought his asthma was something that slowed him down but nothing more. Now, for the first time, he hears from his mother that he could die from it. This was the formative input into Joseph's 'Death Event' (A Death Event is what I think my death will be).

Why did this thought get so concretely set?

Joseph could see two or three reasons.

The first was that his mother revealed his cousin's tragedy to him and had overtly linked it to asthma. Joseph's cousin's condition was very similar to his own, and his mother telling him the cause of his cousin's death meant that it was important to her that Joseph knew about it.

Second, his mother often revelled in the tragedy surrounding death (something Joseph felt was inherent in her culture – she would never miss a funeral, no matter how tenuous her connection to the deceased), the impression being that people who suffer great tragedy are special.

Piecing these jigsaw pieces together, Joseph's mind revealed his (hereto invisible) belief that 'My mother wants me to die, in the same way as my cousin' (so she can revel in the drama surrounding the death – she may not actually have had this thought, but for Joseph this appeared to be the case, and remember, that's what matters).

Joseph mulled over a few other possible inputs but none seemed as influential or as helpful in Finishing-off this thinking as the two aforementioned. Joseph continued asking questions about his thinking, in particular, he continued with the question, 'Why do I have this thinking?'.

This went on for some considerable time (deeply embedded thinking is so invisible, so deep in the murky part of the pool, that it can take some time to surface... this is where it helps to be patient) without much success. This was easily long enough for him to give up, but persevere he did, and one day some seemingly unrelated thinking started to provoke his interest.

The thinking that surfaced was something that he had long-known he had, but it had never appeared to be important. Joseph knew he had the Purpose to be 'secure' by avoiding uncertain situations – and as he looked further into this, he realised that the Complex had deeper implications than he first thought. Joseph realised that he was so frightened of something unpleasant happening to him, that his life had become a series of obstacles that he had to overcome and survive. The name of this Purpose is 'I want to die having survived'. This means to get through one's life without suffering (in this case, humiliation) in most, if not all, of life's situations – to have 'survived' them. This thinking had been repeatedly surfacing in Joseph's mind in recent weeks and he knew to look closer at it.

That's when it hit him.

Joseph realised that, if he has (and likely had for a very long time) a Purpose 'to die having survived', then 'being alive' is an obstacle to his Purpose. In other words, another reason for dying (in this case) from a heart attack would be to expedite achieving his Purpose – that of dying to avoid all of life's possible humiliations.

Perhaps take a moment to process that.

...

...

Right, let's keep going...

'To die having survived' had always been in Joseph's thinking, although invisibly, and even though it took a long time for Joseph to see it, eventually he did. Often, thoughts that are deeper in the pool take longer to surface.

Watching our thinking (in tandem with Going Limp, as opposed to judging or punishing ourselves for having the Unfinished Thinking) has the effect of gently teasing apart the components of the Complex, and increasingly weakening it.

Most people spend their lives losing themselves from the questions they have about their lives.

> *"Advice is what we ask for when we already*
> *know the answer but wish we didn't"*
> *Erica Jong[7]*

To change the way we think we have to stop losing ourselves from the questions we have, and then ask further questions which come from the answers we were avoiding.

"A problem shared is a problem halved."

What is the basis of this well-known saying?

It's that the act of sharing our thoughts/problems etc. lessens their effect on us. By sharing, we reduce the amount of stress or suffering we have and it opens up the possibility of us overcoming our issues. This book is written to enable you (by understanding the way the mind works) to free yourself from a lifetime of unwanted thoughts and feelings. Talking to someone about your life and what you are finding out about yourself makes the process of FoffTing even more effective. For those of you who are interested in more structured help there are workshops available – please go to the link at the back of the book for more details.

3. Foreburning

We've talked about Going Limp and about using it in tandem with other tools. An extremely effective combination to use is Going Limp as part of a Foreburn, but first let's look at what a Foreburn is.

In Chapter Three (Events) we discussed Anticipation. This is when we know there is an Event coming up, like an interview or a wedding or just meeting a friend, and as the Event gets closer we increasingly think about how it will be. This is a naturally occurring phenomenon and people do this all the time; be it a child anticipating dessert at the end of a meal, a boxer preparing for a fight or a teenager going on a date.

What do we do when we Anticipate?
How do we prepare for new or familiar situations?
What tools do we use?

What we tend to do is refer to previous experiences which were the same or similar to the upcoming Happening. If the upcoming Happening is completely new, we refer to an occasion where we experienced something that we consider similar.

As we now know, our experiences shape how we view our life, people and ourselves today, which means we Anticipate future Happenings based on our established Mindprints. In the examples above, for instance, 'Ice-cream is joy' for the child anticipating dessert, 'Men are vicious' for the boxer preparing for a fight, and likely, 'Men/women are titillating' for the teenager heading out on a date.

So, what do we tend to do when there is an upcoming Happening?

You probably start by visibly thinking about what you *physically* want to do and what your intentions are, but intentions aren't what dictate your behaviour they are only what we'd *prefer* the outcome to be. What dictates *all* behaviour are Purposes and Mindprints.

Anticipation is the preparation for a Happening you are about to have, based on how things have happened in the *past*, regardless of any unique circumstances *now*. Anticipation is preparing your state of mind based on your Mind Erosion.

When you Anticipate, you decide what your Purposes are going to be, what Actions you will use to achieve them and what elements of your Mindprint will be influencing you. Take the boy who is anticipating his date, he might have grown up with sisters who regularly teased him which formed a particular Women Event. In this case it means his Anticipation of the date is influenced by the Women Event 'Women are humiliating'. Alternatively, he may have a sister that helped their mother to raise the family and so his Anticipation might include 'Women care' or even 'Caring women are titillating'. Or if he had a sister who he played with a lot – 'Women belong'.

So, based on past experiences your mind actively influences your Anticipation for the same situations to occur. In this way we reinforce what we think life is – and this is why people often say, 'I knew that was going to happen' after an Event. Well, yes, you did know because you (unawarely) planned it. You fitted the new situation to how your previous situations went because this is habitual, preferred and more comfortable and secure than any other outcome.

A Foreburn, however, is *visible* Anticipation – and this (literally) changes everything! A Foreburn is where we *visibly design* the thinking we want to have in an upcoming situation and then frequently and repetitively (you can remind yourself from Chapter Five – Formation of Consciousness) prepare this state of mind so that, when the time comes, the Complex has been set. If this work is done frequently and repetitively enough, we can have any state of mind we choose in any situation.

This is how we can start to change our thinking so that it is to our benefit rather than 'it' controlling our lives to our detriment.

Foreburn
Aware Anticipation

Let's look at some specific circumstances. Public speaking consistently comes top of the list of people's greatest fears. Philip is a teacher at a children's stage school where he occasionally addresses large groups of parents to introduce the students' end of term presentations. Philip knows that his pattern is to get very nervous as he takes his place centre stage. He always delivers his words, but inside his head is a whirlwind, his body and face tense up with fear and his hands shake so much that he has to keep moving to avoid people noticing this. It's a very unpleasant experience which Philip wants to stop repeating.

To fully explain what Philip did to change you will need the details of how Philip applied Foreburning; how he used his imagination awarely rather than leave his Mind Erosion to dictate this situation.

Several times a day, every day for two weeks before the day of the presentation, Philip imagines himself on stage at the end of term review. He imagines the entire scene, as though he is there, looking through his eyes, and imagining all the sense data of the environment – the voices, sounds, smell, atmosphere and temperature of the room. This is important as in the same way a smell or song can bring back a memory, sense data in your Foreburn will it help it 'stick'. Philip imagines looking at the sea of parents' expectant faces…here, he immediately starts to feel fear and his mind begins to speed up. At this point, Philip would normally want to lose himself but instead he relaxes his body and relaxes on this feeling of fear (Go Limp). By Going Limp Philip has created space in his head to continue with this work and imagine the audience interested in everything he says, including some people gently nodding. While doing this, Philip also brings in the impression of enjoying himself while talking to them. (This is easy to do, just think of something you really enjoy and allow this to fill your head and use that impression as you picture your scene). This impression is the Purpose 'I want to enjoy my time'. To top it all off Philip also spends a little time practising what he is going to say out loud while thinking these impressions. Later the same day Philip runs through the same thing, letting the fear come (and if it does), Going Limp, and then bringing in the same pictures and impressions while saying the things he planned to say.

And that's it!

The trick, if there is one, is to Foreburn often enough without forcing, just gently allow it to be there, several times a day, every day, for (in this case) two weeks.

The day of the presentation arrives. Philip is sitting with the students facing the stage, behind him he hears mutterings from the expectant audience entering the hall to find their seats. Philip begins to feel nervous, his gut tightens and his mind has started to race. 'Oh Shit! I shouldn't be feeling nervous! What if the Foreburn hasn't worked?!'. 'Well', he thought, 'if it hasn't worked I might as well know how bad it is' and Philip turns around to look at the audience to see how this makes him feel. As he does, to Philip's surprise, he finds his nerves subsiding and the impression of enjoyment entering his head.

At the appropriate time, Philip gets up, takes his place on stage and starts his presentation, with this same impression of enjoyment remaining his head.

His Foreburn *had* worked!

Why these initial nerves though?
It was because rather than seeing the audience face-on, they were walking in *behind* him. During the two weeks of Foreburning, Philip's mental pictures (that he had created with his imagination) were of the audience in front of him, looking at him – not walking behind him. The Complex could, therefore, only 'kick in' once the audience were in front of him. Looking at the stage head on, Philip felt shaky with nerves (as he usually did), again because the Complex he had created had not yet implemented. However, once he was looking out at the crowd, as he had prepared, the Foreburn was successful. From this day on Philip's presentations have been a much more pleasant experience.

The process of using your imagination to Foreburn is effective; however, time and consideration do need to be invested for the Foreburn to work. Put the time in and you'll get your results.

The most useful Foreburn you can do at this stage is when you're faced with circumstances which you find difficult, stressful or unpleasant. Here, Foreburn Going Limp – so that you create the Complex of Going Limp when the unpleasant situation arises. Do what Philip did – imagine you are in the difficult situation and bring in the impression of Going Limp, letting go of the stress that's there.

A step further is to Go Limp on a particular sensation. For instance, if you know that with certain people or in a particular situation you feel frustration, then during your Foreburn bring to mind the impression of frustration (thinking about past occasions with sense data will do this) and then Go Limp on it.

Being more specific with your Foreburns, will make the results more substantial and you will have greater confidence to handle whatever comes up. Do this frequently and repetitively, at least three or four times a day for a week or two, and see what happens. If it doesn't work for you the first time, increase the number of times you Foreburn. With practice, you won't need to do as much work (not that spending time 'imagining' is such hard work), but the mental 'effort' you put in at the beginning may seem more than further down line, when your Complex for this 'work' has been created.

4. Foreburning and The Juggernaut Metaphor

Do you notice that your thinking can vary in its speed? It might be that in the mornings you recognise your thinking as slow or calm? Perhaps you notice you have faster thinking on mornings when there is an important Event that day? You may recognise this as an anxiousness about getting on with the day.

The reason why our thinking speeds up varies. There are times when we need our thinking to be faster or slower depending on the situation. You may need a faster speed of thinking to quickly orientate e.g. when playing sports, and a slower speed when contemplating an idea. No one speed is 'right', however, if it's too fast too often, regardless of the circumstances, then there is something wrong.

Perhaps you recognise times when your thinking becomes noticeably faster for no reason. You see your mind jumping from one thought to another without being able to control it. It can be that you have become so accustomed to this speed of thinking, that you don't notice it anymore or when you do notice it, your Adjusters tell you it is a virtue to be such a quick thinker. If any of this applies to you, you will likely have found some areas of this book irritatingly pedantic or laborious; places where we have slowed you down to walk you through an important concept. For you, these were ideas you picked up easily; however, that doesn't mean you understood (let alone integrated) them. It's just that you told yourself you did…and quickly read on.

Something to (slowly) ponder.

Fast thinking is usually there to avoid thinking something; it's to lose yourself, because when your mind is racing it's difficult to see what's bothering you. Fast thinking, therefore, affects your Awareness and makes it impossible to change unwanted Complexes.

One of the main reasons why people find it hard to change their Complexes is because their thinking is too fast to allow any change. When an opportunity to change a thought-pattern arises, their thinking is so fast that the opportunity goes before there is the chance to do anything. We don't notice our fast thinking we only notice the missed opportunities.

Clive works in an office and often wants to get straight into his work to meet the deadlines that regularly come up. Unfortunately (for Clive), he often gets caught up in gossiping with colleagues around the coffee station at the beginning of the day. Every day he finds this difficult to avoid. Each day he regrets doing it but the next day he finds himself standing there again, chatting away.

Metaphorically this situation is like a Juggernaut (big articulated lorry) hurtling down the motorway fast lane, where the change of thinking/behaviour you want to implement is a turning off the motorway. The Juggernaut is going too fast to change lanes and take the turn off, and you only have time to glance to the side as the junction flashes by.

The only way to make a change is to slow down. These days we are accustomed to living fast-paced lives and we often complain, blaming 'modern day' for our inability to slow down and stop to think. However, it isn't the pace of our lives that's the problem – it's the speed of our thinking. The Juggernaut is a metaphor for our thinking being too fast and the need for it to slow down to change our patterns.

Without slowing down our thinking, we have no chance of changing anything!

To give ourselves the opportunity for change, we need to slow down enough to see the junction approaching, change gear, change lanes and pull off onto the slip road.

For Clive, this involves planning – Foreburning what he wants to do/think in every moment of his morning so that, as the time approaches, when he would normally lose himself in needless chat, his thinking is prepared to take a different course of action. For instance, Clive Foreburns the moment just before walking into his office so that his thoughts are slow enough that he can keep his attention on getting to his desk. He Foreburns making his cup of coffee whilst keeping his thinking slow, which will enable him to keep his attention on leaving the coffee station as soon as it is done. Clive Foreburns what to say if he feels he is being engaged in needless conversation. By slowing down his thinking enough Clive is successful at making his desired changes.

Foreburning works, if it doesn't for you there is a reason why. Perhaps you didn't Foreburn frequently or repetitively enough, or your mental pictures and impressions while you were Foreburning were that of failing: 'I'll do it but it probably won't work'.

For Foreburns to work you need to be very honest with your Afterburns.

When done correctly, Foreburns always work.

EXERCISE 7

Try Foreburning something uncomplicated to see how this works. Think of a situation that for some reason you don't enjoy but also one that doesn't matter too much to you. You're looking for circumstances that come up regularly but aren't especially important e.g. approaching someone attractive in a bar, speaking to your child's teacher or asking help from a 'moody' colleague. Then, for at least five days beforehand, several times a day, imagine yourself in that situation (remember to include all the sense data of the room, people, etc.) relaxing mentally and physically on what would be your normal stresses – in other words to Go Limp.
See what happens!

5. Afterburn

We covered Afterburning in Events. This is where you look to see what happened after an Event to see what thoughts you had during it. Did I manage to do what I planned? Was there anything wrong with what or the way I Foreburned? What was it that caused my thoughts to run away with me? What do I regret doing? What helped me? What could I have done differently? During an Afterburn you retrace the train of thoughts you had during an Event and see if you can improve things.

Afterburn
Aware Dissipation

In many respects a good Afterburn doubles as a good (initial) Foreburn because during your Afterburn you are deciding what you want to think next time.

Make Afterburns a regular practice and you will see how effectively they increase your Awareness. Contemplating Events after they have happened,

175

rather than helplessly/aimlessly moving (and rushing) from Event to Event will reduce the likelihood of creating further Unfinished Thinking and will instil the useful Complex of FoffTing instead.

6. I want to want...

What do you do when nothing works?

You have some thinking which you know you don't want to have but which feels strongly hooked in. You don't appear to have the visible will to do anything about this thinking or you may feel apathy towards it. The extreme of this – and the clearest example of these types of thoughts – are addictions and compulsions. Strong Complexes are the same as addictions, they just don't manifest as obviously. In these situations, when you feel there is nothing you can do, use, 'I want to want...'.

Let's say you want to stop your compulsion of buying a chocolate bar everyday as you travel home from work, which has become your pattern. You look toward the end of the day with uncertainty as to whether you will be able to walk past the confectioners without going in, knowing that you have never been able to before, no matter how hard you tried. Chances are you won't this time either, you want to change but don't have the will to do so.

Question: What is 'will'? What does it mean to have the will to do something you visibly want to? What makes anyone do anything?

Answer: Having a Purpose i.e. pictures and/or impressions of achieving that thing.

When we say we have no will, we mean we have no Purpose (to achieve the thing in question) or the Purpose is overwhelmed by another Purpose – 'I want to fail'. So, to have the will to do something, we have to develop the Purpose to achieve the thing we want. But(!) because the Purpose to fail can be very strong, developing this new Purpose can usually only be done in small increments over time. Bit by bit, little by little, the Purpose to do the thing we want grows until one day...ta daaa! It is there.

'I want to want...' works like a request you make to yourself to want to have the will to stop buying the chocolate bar sometime in the future. You know you don't have the strength now, but by putting in a request each time you think about chocolate you will eventually have your new Purpose.

Let's say around mid-morning the image or impression of eating chocolate comes to mind, with it probably comes an impression of not being able to stop, maybe even some despair. When this happens, think to yourself, 'I want to want to stop eating chocolate'...and an hour later when you are thinking about the shop, think, 'I want to want to walk past the shop'... keeping this up whenever a 'chocolate thought' comes into your head.

With 'I want to want...' it's important that you don't put any timescale or pressure on yourself to achieve this change. Simply keep asking your Consciousness to 'want to want...' to change the way you think. If you are working with a particularly strong Complex you won't be able to change immediately, and that's OK, there is no need to judge yourself whatever the outcome. If you keep using, 'I want to want...' frequently and repetitively, eventually a Purpose will begin to develop and become important to you and your mind will have created the will to walk past.

The example here is chocolate but it can be anything because the specifics are irrelevant. Whether it's giving up chocolate, or any pattern of thinking or behaviour you have, use FRT to request the will and the Purpose will emerge.

'I want to want...' is your Back Line of Defence. It means even when you have no will to stop now you can always 'I want to want...' and in time, in the near future, it will become a Purpose.

Chapter Nine
FoffTing Questions and Tools

In the previous chapter we covered Going Limp, Watching Our Thinking, Foreburns, Afterburns and 'I want to want' – all of which are useful FoffTing strategies.

However, if you genuinely want to change the way you think you'll need to get to the very *core* of what you're working with, to thoroughly root it out. For this, most of your time will initially be spent isolating and identifying the *origins* of your Unfinished Thinking. We've repeatedly emphasised how asking questions is a fundamental tool to unravelling your thinking. *Which* questions, is the focus of this chapter.

There are an infinite number of questions you could ask about why you think what you think, so what follows is a framework to get you started and guide you forward. Don't think that you need to be FoffTing while you read this chapter because at first it will be useful just to have an overview, and later you can revisit this chapter as necessary with specific Unfinished Thinking that you would like to Finish-off.

The following three questions are the main framework for your exploration. These questions lead to further off-shoot questions, which we will come to.

1. What have I got? (or what is the thought/thinking that I want to Finish-off?)

2. How did it get there? (How did it originate? (What experiences led to its formation?)

3. What is it doing to my life? (How are these thoughts affecting my life now and what will they do to my future?)

Aside from this outline, there is no fixed route to follow. Simply give yourself time with each of the question areas, see what emerges... and go with the momentum.

Alternatively, when something is on your mind that you want to 'investigate', remind yourself of these questions, see which one provokes your interest the most, and use this as an indication of where to start.

1. What have I got?

We've acknowledged that by reading this book you will already have thoughts that are nagging at you to be explored. If this is the case that's great, but you may also be sat there thinking, 'I now know I have a lot of stuff in my head and I can't fathom where to start' (with subsequent thoughts of, 'Get me a drink...', 'Where are my cigarettes?...', 'I'll just check my phone...').

It can be difficult to get started but usually only at first. Your mind has likely developed efficient ways of bypassing this kind of probing. You may recall having an experience of deciding to resolve a situation by doing a little contemplation in the evening. However, when you arrive home you find yourself 'needing' a cup of tea first, then a few hours later you're brushing your teeth, facing yourself in the mirror and the fact that you never 'got around to' doing what you had intended. You then think, 'Oh well, there's always tomorrow' and you switch out the light.

One way to solve this problem is to start now, that's NOW now (not tomorrow now, or in ten minutes now! but NOW!). To do this you (very simply) ask yourself:

- *What am I thinking about now?*
- *What is bothering me?*

By answering either of these questions immediately after asking them, you will side-step the *Bodyguards* that would normally take you off track.

Bodyguards?

Yes, this very aptly named group of thoughts are ones that 'protect' thinking you have. Bodyguards prevent your probing mind from going anywhere near the thoughts in their protection and will greatly resist you wanting to dis-member established patterns.

Bodyguards can be Adjusters (described in the Mindprint chapter) e.g. "I've got too much to do tonight", "I'd love to but…". They can also have physical effects like drowsiness, irritability, headaches or mental effects like confusion or numbness. Bodyguards can surface as thoughts about what you are doing, 'Yes that's all well and good, but I really need to… do something else that is more 'important' than changing my thinking…'.

Bodyguards are usually the Purpose, 'I want to fail' working at its finest.

However they manifest, Bodyguards are designed to keep your Mind Erosion intact.

Don't let them win!

OK – back to our questions,

- *What am I thinking about now?*
- *What is bothering me?*

By acquiring the habit of asking questions and pursuing your answers, Bodyguards will gradually stop interfering. As they dissipate, they clear the way for you to become more aware of the invisible thoughts that you have been protecting yourself from. With the space clear to see what's been in the Bodyguards custody, you may be surprised how often you think some of these, now nagging thoughts.

Another good question to ask is:

- *What am I avoiding thinking about?*

Often a recent Event can bother us but we allow it to sit in our mind as background noise; it might be a call or an email we've received or an ongoing problem at home. Sometimes it's simply something someone said that won't stop niggling us. Whatever it is, we often avoid it and get on with our daily lives while this background noise buzzes around the back of our heads, contributing to our 'bad mood' and making us suffer (your words to describe it may be, "I feel distracted… annoyed… uncomfortable… stressed… angry… unsettled…" but you can't say exactly why). This thinking is often easily perceivable, only requiring us to stop what we're doing for a moment and ask, *What am I avoiding thinking about?* to make it visible. If you do this, and take a little time for a bit more thought, you will likely to finish it off and be able to get on with your life with a clear head.

If you're having trouble with the questions in this chapter so far, try these more visible thoughts to get you started:

- *What do I repeatedly think?*
- *What thoughts regularly occupy my mind?*
- *What are my daydreams?*
- *Do they follow a pattern?*

Daydreams, for instance, usually exist because we think we can't achieve the things we dream about – someone who frequently dreams of being rich might have the Self Event 'I am a Failure'.

Another inroad to your Unfinished Thinking is to find something from everyday life that you wouldn't expect to examine. For example:

- *What expressions do I repeatedly use?*
- *Why do I use these expressions rather than others?*

Expressions are visible thoughts which stick in your mind (more than others) because they match the invisible thoughts in your Mindprint. Looking at the phrases you repeatedly say can reveal what you are repeatedly thinking. Notice which expressions you use or come to mind easily, this will help you find out which Mindprint elements they correlate to.

"No pain, no gain" is a common phrase but what's the thinking behind it?

The accepted understanding is 'Only hardworking people succeed'. But the phrase clearly has the impression of needing to endure pain, hardship, suffering etc. for success. It also means that a person doesn't think they *can* succeed *without* pain/hardship/suffering so they will eventually 'create' difficulties so that success may come as a result.

Here are a few more:
- "The grass is always greener on the other side" (I can't be satisfied, Life is a disappointment)
- "Beggars can't be choosers" (Inferior people can't have a life)
- "Don't wash your dirty linen in public" or "Don't let the cat out of the bag" (these usually stem from the family environment and are designed to keep family Shame Events undiscovered)

It's worth considering that just because these sayings have been used for years does not mean they are helpful to you or your life. There are some sayings that are encouraging like, "Every cloud has a silver lining" – but there are others that are not, like "Life is a shit sandwich".

The point is to ask questions about the many influences on your thinking that have (somewhat comfortably) remained unexamined.

When you start with frequent expressions, memories, specific thoughts, or whatever it is you would like to know more about, you simply need to keep asking yourself questions (and look for answers! Don't lose yourself and move on to the next question and then head for a cup of coffee...).

Often, as we've looked at before, seemingly unrelated thoughts are connected. That's why useful questions to delve deeper are:

- *What other thoughts are in my head at the same time?*
- *Why are they there together at the same time?*
- *What is the relationship between them?*

If thoughts surface together, they are connected and are either part of the same Complex or closely connected Complexes, even if it might not be obvious how.

You may be looking at a strong visible thought that's been holding your attention like, 'Jerry is a bully', 'That shopkeeper always overcharges' or 'I do like a good cup of tea' or 'Fucking traffic…'. When you identify one clear visible thought immediately ask, *What is the VTA for this thought?* And then look at the VTA elements behind this thought.

- *What just happened that made me see these thoughts?*

…is a helpful question to ask to identify the 'seemingly' random or irrelevant circumstances that can be part of the Complex – another clue in the investigation!

In the last chapter, we discussed the propensity to fool ourselves or to complacently think we are right in thinking what we do, and earlier in this chapter we talked about Bodyguards – these are the tactics we use to resist changing our thoughts. The Mind/Mind Erosion wants (because of the comfort and security we feel) to ensure its own survival and will try to fool itself whenever it needs to. Stubbornly sticking to one point of view no matter what others say or evidence to the contrary, is another good indication of the same attachment 'to security' and the 'comfort of how things have always been'. When you catch yourself being single-minded in this way, take the opportunity to see if what you think is really just the visible, and if so (and it usually is) what the invisible is underneath it. Remember the invisible is contradictory to the visible. So, look for what would be the opposite of the visible that you've identified. Make sure you do this within the context of your mind rather than in an academic way. You're looking for what the opposite would be for *your* Consciousness (we will also look at Derek's example later):

- *What if this is just what I want to believe, what if this is just a visible thought?*
- *And therefore, what would be the opposite of this for me.*

The strength of our attachment to what we think is an indicator of our Unfinished Thinking. Surely an open mind would not be concerned with what is right but be willing to question.

Look at the logic of what you think, try explaining your point of view to someone and see if there are issues with your logic – it may be that your logic is very thin:

- *What would be a more accurate explanation for why I am thinking what I am thinking?*

By 'more accurate', we are directing you to the root of the thinking; asking you to go deeper and be more honest with yourself no matter how (at first) unnerving it may be.

> *"The truth will set you free, but first it will piss you off"*
> *Anon.[8]*

You will know when you have reached the truth because it will 'feel right' and probably a little uncomfortable too. To go straight to the core ask:

- *What is the most laughter-, cringe- or anger-provoking explanation for these thoughts?*

"I notice I get angry at the slightest suggestion that I am perceived to be a failure/stupid/lonely" etc. "If I think I am behaving like my mum, it makes me cringe and to think that I might be recreating her life makes me feel sick".

These reactions indicate that you're getting real answers.

Watch out for fooling yourself though – it's easy to say things like "No that's not it, I'm fine" or "That doesn't really bother me" – when underneath there is something unfinished lingering.

Finding Labels

As you repeat this process, impressions and thoughts will come to you. To isolate what you want to focus on you need to find the right name for it. These are not just any names or ones you are 'comfortable' with (remember the warning we gave in Mindprint). The aim is to isolate the things that bother you and identify what they really are. You need to look for (key) words which definitively sum up (and therefore, unlock) what you really think about life, people, yourself, etc. Like Rumpelstiltskin, only by finding the right names can you be free of these thoughts.

Linda knows that her Self Event bothers her and she knows it's roughly to do with the feeling she gets whenever she makes mistakes, which for her seem all too often. She eventually identifies the thought 'I'm stupid', but while it logically makes sense it leaves her with doubt. Then the word 'retard' pops into her mind and she begins to cry. Linda knows this is the word that matches the impression she's had about herself all her life. For some people 'retard' is a word that shouldn't be used anymore because it can cause upset and is politically incorrect, however, it *is* the word which Linda's Consciousness finds as a match for the thinking she has. With the precise key in the lock, the door to her Unfinished Thinking has opened and allowed her to really see/feel/understand the full extent/depth of her Unfinished Thinking about herself.

When you find the right word to your Unfinished Thinking you go from logically reasoning the subject, to getting the full sense data about it; how you feel about yourself, your life or whatever it is that has bothered you for so long. This initiates an enormous catharsis and you literally feel unlocked! For Linda, her tears were a result of feeling this catharsis. Without identifying the precise label Linda would still be living with confusion and frustration.

If you want to find out what you really think about your life, yourself and others you have to find *the* words which match the thinking you have.

It's very easy to Finish-off comfortable things e.g. 'The cake didn't taste good this time because I put in too many eggs, next time I'll put in less'.

There, easily done.

However what is more helpful is to look for what we are *avoiding* to look at – perhaps 'I put in too many eggs because... actually, I always do. Well, why do I always do that? What happens when I do that... I notice that I feel humiliated because I often tell others how good I am at making cakes. Oh shit, maybe being humiliated is my Purpose?!'

Certainly, finding out that you 'want to be humiliated' is an uncomfortable endpoint and yet it's a far more productive endpoint than comfortably sitting in your Mind Erosion feeling humiliated all the time. With your life exactly as it has always been, where you're wishing it was otherwise.

Perhaps you are having trouble finding out what Purpose you have, if so ask the following to walk yourself towards it:

- *What pay-off can I expect by thinking these thoughts?*
- *What can I expect to achieve by thinking/behaving like this?*

And therefore:

- *What is my Purpose?*

2. How did it get there?

The next step is to see where this thinking started and how it developed. Whatever thoughts you are looking at, they most probably started in your childhood so a good question to ask is:

- *Does this thinking link to my earliest memories, my EA?*
- *What other memories come to mind?*

Remember Joseph from the Watching Our Thinking section in the last chapter? Joseph's relationships with women had always suffered from arguments and friction, and then he saw that part of the reason was his thought 'Women want me to fail'. Joseph always thought 'Women want me to fail' was an isolated Women Event (there's no such thing) until he asked himself whether his Women Event had any connection to an EA...

When...BAM!

He saw it.

Remember Joseph's memory of his mother telling him about the death of his cousin because of his asthma? Remember Joseph questioning why his mother had said this to him when he too had asthma? Looking at these thoughts in this moment Joseph saw that this EA was at the core of his Women Event, 'Women make me fail!'.

Reading this you might think, 'Now that I hear it, it seems obvious, why didn't he notice it before?'. The thing is when it's *your* own thoughts, these associations, no matter how obvious, remain hidden from you – 'hidden in plain sight' you could say. You need to ask questions for the connections to become visible and this is what finishes them off.

You now know that we go through life with our childhood Events continuously influencing our adult experiences, which in turn strengthens those (early set) Complexes. Knowing this, we can then ask:

- *What other Events in my adult life could be connected to (or have influenced) these thoughts?*
- *How has this Complex strengthened over the years?*

From the Mindprint chapter you understand the nature and importance of Shame Events and the destructive influence they have on our lives. So, if you haven't already done so, take a deep breath and ask yourself to honestly answer:

- *What are my most shameful thoughts?*
- *What do I least want people to know about me? i.e. what are my Shame Events?*

We all have things we are ashamed of doing and perhaps the first memories to surface here will be from your adult life. Look at those first. These adult Shame Events, although cringy, will not be the real cause of your unhappiness – but they will be a good place to start and something you can tackle in preparation for the ones which will need a little more courage.

To find the roots of your issues you need to look into your childhood and your EAs:

- *What Shame Events did I get from my EA and other memories/experiences?*

Shame and the family are closely linked, inseparable in fact. So, to deal with your most shameful thoughts you will need to look at your family life, the behaviour of your parents, the thoughts you had about them and thoughts you picked up from them. Remember these are just thoughts, they also happen to be obstructing you living a fulfilled life, that's why we are going through this – not to humiliate you or make you suffer.

- *What are the most shameful thoughts I have about my parents/family?*
- *What thoughts would I least like to admit to myself and others that I think about my parents/family?*

If diving in at the deep end with the above questions is too difficult, start with:

- *What do I hate most in the visible behaviour of my parents?*

And

- *Why?*

Another useful approach to assessing your thinking is to look at your Pride Events. We tend to think positive thoughts about ourselves to cover up our shame, this is how shame and pride go hand in hand; interlocked, with the Pride Event protecting the Shame Event. To find your shame first identify your Pride Event. Derek will help us explain:

Derek is a delivery driver and prides himself on being able to drive, read a map and eat a sandwich at the same time. His feeling is that this is a skill others don't have. His Pride Event is, 'I am a good driver'.

This isn't to say that you shouldn't take pride in something about yourself or something you have done. It's just if your mind is attached to this pride, it suggests it's a Pride Event. Start with:

- *What are my Pride Events?*
- *What is it I want people to know/think about me?*

Once you find a Pride Event then ask:

- *What is the shame underneath it?*

As a clue, remember that the visible Shame Event usually directly contrasts the invisible Pride Event, and always in the context of the persons thinking i.e. an individual sees the Pride/Shame Events as opposites but others may not agree — and that doesn't matter.

So, if Derek's Pride Event is, 'I'm a good driver' what would his Shame Event be?

'I'm a bad driver?

But that sounds dumb.

Derek could have stopped here but instead he kept thinking about it until it clicked for him: 'What kind of life do I have if being a good driver is what I am proud of?'

It hit him like a punch in the stomach (a good indication). Derek realised that if something as mundane as driving is his Pride, then his Shame (*he thinks*) is 'I have no life'.

Seeing, considering and, particularly sharing our Shame Events with others are the best ways of FoffTing that there is. Derek's Shame Event might seem heavy (although, it is common) but the relief and the lightness he felt afterwards was palpable — as it will be for you).

The sense of relief that comes with discovering and sharing Shame Events is nothing new. As we touched on earlier, the phrase 'A problem shared is a problem halved' means this very thing. Although few people fully appreciate its significance and the effect it has on our Consciousness.

3. What is it doing to my life?

This final section of questions looks at what the Unfinished Thoughts are doing to your life now and in the future.

It is essential to look at how your Unfinished Thinking affects the way you live on a daily basis; how it influences your perception of the world, your preferences, habits, your regrets and missed opportunities etc.

- *What influence did my Unfinished Thinking have on the experiences I've had?*
- *How have these thoughts affected my life until now?*

These thoughts might be hard to look at because none of us like to think we've missed out on having a life and even worse, that we were the ones that caused it. By accepting our lives for what they are rather than what we like to think they are, gives us the Purpose to improve our lives enormously.

Kim is an actor with a reasonably successful career but there has always been a nagging thought in her mind that she is 'wary of pushing herself forward'. Kim's impression is that she would rather remain a supporting actor. Giving this further thought, Kim remembers numerous occasions which illustrate how her life could be seen as a series of missed opportunities. No coincidence that five weeks after seeing this thinking she landed her first lead role in a 20-year career.

The next questions to consider would be how these thoughts, if they continue to be thought, will shape the rest of your life:

- *What is the best and the worst that might happen to me if I continue thinking these thoughts?*

Although Mai is an attractive woman she has had very few boyfriends. When asked why she thinks this is the case she replies, "Because I'm fussy". Implying that she is holding out for the right one.

But…

What if she has to wait a long time for the right one?

Or worse, what if he never comes at all.

And what if, 'I'm fussy' is a visible thought anyway? What if her Purpose to have the perfect partner is invisibly a Purpose to have no partner at all?

- *How will these thoughts affect my life if I continue to think them?*
- *What will happen in 20 years' time if I keep thinking as I think now?*
- *What will become of me?*

This line of questioning broadens your perspective on your life – long term, way into the future. Rather than succumbing to a life with this Unfinished Thinking with "It's OK, it doesn't really affect me that much", look at how it will affect your life in the long-term and use that as an impetus to Finishing it off.

- *What if my children pick up these thoughts?*
- *What if, as I have seen with my parents, these thoughts become compounded with age (which is true by the way – ditches get deeper)?*
- *What if, with this thinking (as with the 'fussy' girl), I end up lonely in later life?*
- *What will my regrets be if I continue to think these thoughts?*

The response, 'If I am OK now, why worry about it' is the ostrich with its head in the sand.

Why not take your head out and change your future by doing some simple exercises (which is only to answer a bunch of questions which will reveal more of yourself to you) and actively improve your life now and for the future? Rather than avoiding having a life in both?

191

The questions above are examples of the many that you could ask. What is key to this last of the three main questions – 'What is it doing to my life?' – is that it should give you the motivation to keep going with this work, knowing that you can change your future (little by little, from now).

Wherever you start and with whichever questions you ask, remember FoffTing may at first seem like an effort, confusing or frustrating but eventually the process will open itself up to you.

It will also open you up to yourself.

EXERCISE 8

If you want to have the experience of Finishing-off Thinking or at least have a taste of how it can feel, share with someone an experience you've had that was in some way shameful.

Consider the following for this exercise:
First, who you will tell. It needs to be someone you trust, and someone that will allow you to share with them without you having fear of how they will react. Nor should they have any fear of how you may react e.g. tears or anger.

Next, Foreburn to Go Limp on any fear that might arise, and simply share the Event as it happened without expectation of any specific response from your friend. This is crucial to sharing; you can't want anything from the listener, not forgiveness or sympathy, care or even understanding. Nothing, other than for the friend to listen.

Ideally, the Shame Event that you choose to discuss shouldn't be one that you've told anyone before, nor should it be something too upsetting. In this way, you can have the experience of sharing and minimize the risk of having a negative experience.

This exercise is effective in demonstrating how, as you share, your feeling of shame reduces simply because you are not hiding it (i.e. ashamed of it) anymore.

Certainly, nothing can replace talking to a skilled tutor or experienced counsellor who can observe and comment objectively without Egotistic Purposes i.e. they can give helpful feedback, without wanting to belong or be admired etc. We recommend working with a tutor or attending one of our workshops because the experience of working with others is so beneficial. Having said that, this exercise should illustrate to you the sense of relief and lightness that simple sharing can bring.

Conclusion
Final Guiding Words

It can be disheartening (and for some, depressing) to see how we have *really* lived; the negative repercussions of our early-life Events and regret over the years spent in a slumber to the realities of our thinking.

It is important however, to remember that the past is the past and you can't change it. What you *can do* though, is decide whether to lose yourself from your past (and then, so too from your life), sulk about it (by sitting in your ditch; your Mind Erosion), be angry and resentful about what happened…

…Or you can rethink it all and change the course of all that lies ahead for you!

You see your future is now yours!

You can be who you want to be!

In five or ten years' time, you can either look back with regret about what you didn't do to change, or you can thank yourself that you (bought this book and) took your life in your hands.

In Part One we covered the principal subjects that explain *Why We Think the Way We Do*, including:
- Mind Erosion, and how it wants to think itself irrespective of the circumstances
- Awareness, how much of your invisible thinking you can/can't see
- Purposes, what you think will make you happy regardless of how self-destructive it may be

- Mindprint, your unique collection of important generalised Events about life, people and yourself that instruct the way you live – no matter how out of context
- Shame Events and Unfinished Thinking and how devastating they can be on your life

In Part Two we looked at *How to Change It*:
- Going Limp, mentally relaxing on a thought or impression to release it as an Important Thought
- Afterburn, contemplating an Event after it has happened to see what thinking lead to your Event and how, from this understanding, you can live differently
- Foreburn, preparing a specific state of mind to change otherwise difficult circumstances
- The necessity of asking questions, questions, questions!

The overarching theme of this entire work is Awareness and your willingness to continually develop your understanding of how the mind works.

A few cautionary words do need to be shared though, before you well and truly set off.

This journey won't always be the plainest of sailing.

Sorry, but it's best that you are forewarned (and therefore, forearmed).

Do remember that *your Mind Erosion* is the predominant reason for your resistance to FoffTing. The process outlined in this book will, therefore, need patience because your Mind Erosion wasn't created, and therefore can't be dismantled, overnight. You also need to have a realistic expectation of what is involved in achieving the required changes in your thinking – and therefore, your life.

There will be times when you won't want to Go Limp (this is when your Action is, 'I stand my ground'). This will typically be regarding People Events. It's very common, especially once we've seen our invisible thoughts about people (and PiCs in particular), to have ardent resistance to Finishing-off our thoughts about them. This push-back arises as an impression that can be summarised as, 'Why should I let the bastards get away with it?!' (this won't be a question either – it will be a statement).

Look to see if you have this impression lurking.

Another angle on this impression is, 'If I Go Limp on my thoughts towards the people that did me wrong, they will not suffer for what they did/are doing, and they deserve to!' (accompanied by the thought, 'And I'm right!').

Again, see if you recognise this thought (yes, just a thought!).

Now, you may want to have a laugh to yourself about how the mind works…

…Or you may want to go into deep contemplation and compile a list of evidence against the accused, so that you can keep these thoughts in place, because you *really are right*!

Of course, the latter approach won't help you. These kinds of thoughts trample on any aspiration of wanting to be free. They keep you stuck in rigid Mind Erosions which are far from being any use to you.

If they ever were.

Do you get the gist of what's being emphasised here?
It's the point that we started with way back in the Introduction.
It's that this book will help you understand how your Mind Erosion wants to keep you in your ditches, and that it will make you fail so it can remain as it is.

This is why your attention is being brought back to this.

When you catch yourself in a situation where you don't want 'them' to get away with 'it', you're steadfastly holding on to what you want to think about 'them' and their 'wrongdoings'. This isn't you wanting 'to have a life', this is your Mind Erosion, plain and simply, wanting you 'to fail'.

To see how (objectively speaking) illogical it is to have these thoughts, it may help to remember the saying, *'Resentment is like taking poison and expecting the other person to die'*. You are only hurting yourself by holding on to these thoughts, what happened is in the past, let it go, free yourself (and 'them') and you will be much happier.

Something else to be aware of is that although it may not seem so, we enjoy having the Unfinished Thinking we have because, in a broad sense, we belong with our thinking. We consider our thoughts (whatever they are) 'ours': 'They are my thoughts! They make me, me!!'.

Recall the difference between the child who falls over and is choosing whether to laugh or cry, and the sulky stubborn teenager. Letting go of the importance of our thoughts (to ourselves) is crucial to loosening the intense belonging we have to what we think, and to our comfortable ditches.

On this subject, it is also useful to remember that our thinking is designed to achieve Purposes, which by definition are what *we think* will make us happy. The Mindprint is also *designed* by us (are you getting the picture?) to help achieve these Purposes. You see, we enjoy thinking the way we do (albeit invisibly) and because it's 'us' we think it is the 'right way' to think, it gives us our identity!

Saying that, we reassure you that as you expand your Awareness and Finish-off your Thinking you will still be *you*. You will still be the charming, funny, intelligent, sporty or quirky person you are – only now, you will *also* have far clearer thinking and be easily able to make decisions, that previously you couldn't.

Let's end with a metaphor to illustrate the implications of Finishing-off one's thinking to show how it can, at times, be disorientating.

You will already have recognised that Unfinished Thinking distorts your view of the world making you believe things are normal when they aren't.

Figure 10.1 The houses people live in

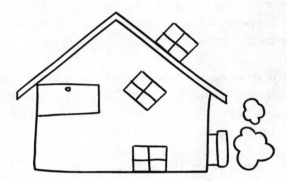

People who have Unfinished Thinking live in houses like the one in Figure 10.1. Their reality is what they think it is, rather than what it is.

> *"A great many people think they are thinking when*
> *they are really rearranging their prejudices"*
> *William James[9]*

People really do think and believe that (for example), 'Life is hard' or they are 'stupid' or that, 'Men are unpredictable' or 'Women are competition' or 'People are out to get them'. They then adjust their perception of the world to fit (these thoughts) the world they have created. This is how/why the house in Figure 10.1 feels right to them.

FoffTing rearranges the various components of the distorted house (Figure 10.1) so that it is functional and conducive to living in (Figure10.2). However, this can feel disorienting at first because things are not where they used to be. This very normal and necessary adjustment period is required for you to adapt to your new life – where life is simply 'what it is'. Here you are free to be whoever you want to be in any moment, and people are just different people, whoever they are in any moment… Rather than Events from your past straight-jacketing you into a contorted view of the world.

Although at first (and it *is* only at first) uncomfortable, this is a great initial stride towards freedom.

Figure 10.2 The house of Finished-off Thinking

Although you may pine for your original house remember, it's just because it's all that you've known, what your Mind Erosion has been comfortable with, don't look back! One of the main reasons people give up when starting to deal with their problems is because of the temporary feeling of insecurity. They give up because something intrinsically doesn't feel right, things are uncomfortable and feel out of place. Whereas these unsettled feelings indicate that they are precisely on track.

Each week Mina is required to make a presentation at a work meeting and these aren't going well. Every time she starts, her thinking speeds up, she gabbles or forgets what she wants to say and has to check her notes. Her performance doesn't threaten her job because otherwise she is very good, but the anxiety surrounding her weekly presentations, is something she would like to be free of. Determined to change the situation, Mina prepares for her next presentation by doing a thorough Foreburn, so that she is completely relaxed and able to Go Limp, leaving her free to focus on what she wants to say. When the day of the next weekly meeting arrives, Mina notices that on her way to the room she feels very relaxed and limp but surprisingly insecure.

Why insecure?
She should feel more confident at this stage.

This 'instability' is, as we've said, because of the changes she's made to her thinking. Mina reminds herself of this and continues to Go Limp. Doing this is all it takes for her to make the required change to deliver her relaxed and successful presentation. Over the next few weeks with equally successful Foreburns/presentations, the insecurity completely faded away

So, don't forget! FoffTing is the same as moving into a new home, things will feel unfamiliar until the new place progressively starts to feel like home. Make sure you give yourself time to adjust to a new way of seeing the world – knowing that this new way is the world as it is.

We recommend you stop here and have a think about (even reread) the paragraphs above from 'plainest of sailing'.

Again, it's important to know the obstacles you may face so that you can be prepared for them.

As we said at the very beginning of this book, your Mind Erosion has become accustomed to being Number One... The Boss... The One Ruling The Joint.

It will want to stay in this Top Dog position and will greatly resist relinquishing control. Watch out for this because this is the difference between success and failure.

Sound serious?

It is.
It's your life.

Ultimately, only *you* are in control of your thinking, you can change how you think but you have to want to, and you have to be honest with yourself.

There is no use Foreburning while thinking, 'This is not going to work' because this is the Purpose, 'I want to fail'. It's also pointless blaming others or circumstances for things that go wrong as, again, this is the Purpose 'I want to fail' – albeit in a weak disguise.

A little more help

Yes, you will hit obstacles to keeping yourself on track, but there's no need to despair. What follows are some helpful tips and phrases that others have found useful.

At times through this process you may feel apprehensive, fearful or even nauseous about going further. This can be for a variety of reasons but predominantly because of a fear that you are going to discover something you don't want to see. When any of these feelings arise, it's useful for you to know that *the fear of seeing the thought is always worse than the thought itself* and what you feel afterwards is only relief and lightness... and disbelief that you've lived with this thought for so long.

Reminder! Reminder! Reminder! *Thoughts are just thoughts* (electrochemistry in the brain) they are not a reflection of reality. Remember – and we repeat this frequently and repetitively for a reason – that just because you always have, you don't need to think one thought any more than another. Let alone *believe* the thoughts you have. If you have a negative thought about yourself it's only a thought, you are not actually what you think you are.

Take a few moments to let that sink in.

...

...

On occasion, obstacles to changing the way you live will surface (the expression 'no one likes change' is common for a reason). The fear is often irrational. If you ask yourself, *What is the worst that can happen?* One of two responses will surface; you will either see that your fears are incredibly unlikely i.e. irrational, or you will see that the worst that could happen is not that bad and your life can continue much the same afterwards.

You may also find that you have fears of things that may or may not ever happen (again an irrational fear). When you recognised this say, *I'll cross that bridge when I reach it'* i.e. I'll sort what needs to be sorted out first and deal with *that,* if and when that happens.

If/when you notice you are fearful of changing a pattern of thinking/ behaviour (despite knowing that this will improve your life), don't put it off! Decide to make the necessary change and carry it out before more obstacles (again, just thoughts) surface – quickly put yourself in a position of no return. Stick to the plan and Go Limp on any feelings of insecurity. Make yourself do what you've decided is right. If you leave things unresolved or to chance, know that you are wanting to fail.

Remember why you are reading this book: It's not to add another tome to your collection of dusty self-help books but to make a difference to your life, for life!

In the course of this work there may be times when you feel upset. This is not a negative thing. Crying with the Action, 'I pity myself' (as opposed to 'I despair') can, in fact, help (unless you get upset at the smallest thing – 'I am sensitive/I want to be special'). When you cry, your vulnerability allows your mind to drop its guard and become more transparent. This opening allows you to see more of what has been hereto invisible. It's also often the case that stress/tension accumulated over many years needs to be released and crying allows this. 'I pity myself' helps to discharge the build-up because you are finally acknowledging your long-endured suffering. Upholding a distorted view of the world leads to an accumulation of mental/emotional stress and physical tension. Crying is like a pressure valve being released which brings much-needed relief and clarity.

If you find yourself despairing at some 'hopeless/painful/suffering' situation (or even this fucking book) say to yourself that *every hopeless situation has at least two solutions.* This is *always* the case. Look for these solutions and see how they can lead you up and out of your despair.

It may be that the Complex you are working with is a strong one, and this will need more time. In this case, your Foreburn may require more attention, detail or practice. Double check that you haven't succumbed to Bodyguards… or losing yourself… or something else. You can only do your best. And If you know you are doing your best you can have peace of mind that you can't do any more. Knowing that you couldn't have done more allows you to let go of self-criticism and worry. If things now don't go the way you wanted, it is no longer down to you.

***

We return to the principal point of this chapter, that change won't always be easy but it *will* be worth it.

This process of increasing your Awareness and FoffTing your Unfinished Thinking is an ongoing one. These are life skills. Know that wherever you are in that process is where you are at that time – it's not a race. You are acquiring an expertise that will transform the rest of your life, it will take time and you will need you to accept that you won't be able to run before you can walk. You didn't learn to read by speed-reading your school books nor learn to drive by navigating a busy city centre, so why rush the most important thing in your life – your life.

You may think that if you take time to contemplate your life, then you have to put it on hold; that other people are getting ahead while you are crawling through the analysis of your thoughts. But deep down you *know* that that you can't 'get on' with your life while you're frustrated, confused, suffering etc. And while other people appear to be galloping ahead into the light of 'success', they are more than likely living with the same kind of problems you are.

To reiterate (because it's critical), changing your life will require you to be transparently honest with yourself.

Look for what makes you react, laugh/cringe/makes you angry or is something you quickly reject/despair at the thought of having. Look at anything which provokes a reaction in you. A reaction means a thought has been provoked that is important to you and while your thoughts are still important to you, this is an indication of Unfinished Thinking. Pay particular attention to the logic of your explanations, if your answers are vague or don't make sense then you may be avoiding something.

You may have had some significant realisations whilst reading this book and this should encourage you that you are on your way to greater Awareness, and the freedom to live as you visibly want to.

***

We acknowledge that by talking about the possible setbacks (above), we risk putting you off doing anything at all (other than enthusiastically throwing this book at the wall). This is because quick and easy fixes are what humans have become used to. Investing time into something in this fast-paced world is rare.

Yet consider this – What are you going to do with your time otherwise?

Watch television?
Read the newspaper?
Daydream?
Listen to music?
Check if you have had a message?
Write a message so that you can get a message?
Open a can of beer?
Have a conversation in your head?
Chat with your neighbour about the weather/the news/the neighbourhood/sport/something you day-dreamed or read somewhere, over a can of beer whilst listening to music, with the television on in the background?

And look! You have a message.
(Good thing you wrote one earlier.)

Now… what was it you were thinking?

There are lots of things you can do to lose yourself from your problems – which we hope you now know, means you simultaneously lose yourself from your life.

Why not do something to *improve* your life instead?

Why not slowly but consistently take steps towards understanding the way you think?

The more FoffTing you do, the more space you will acquire in your head to think the thoughts you want. You will be able to hold your attention on what you are doing without background noise or confusion. You will always be finding out about yourself and increasingly experience states of spontaneity and inspiration.

FoffTing gives you the gift of nulling the all-too-common old-age regret of having lived the way you did, wishing it had been different.

Give yourself the experience of reaching your old age feeling that your life was fulfilled, with gratitude to yourself for what you did to get there.

If you do the work honestly your dedication will be rewarded.

It is within your power to live the life you truly and freely want to live.

Self-discovery is an endlessly-fascinating journey and it's all about you.

What better way to spend your time?

Appendix One
List of Purposes and their Definitions

I want to HAVE A LIFE
I want PiCs to care for me in a way that will make me capable of living my life to the full.

I want to KNOW HOW TO THINK
I want to acquire a consciousness that reflects, rather than constructs/distorts, the outside world, including the thinking of other people. As a result, I will be able to make decisions.

I want to be LOVED
I want other people to think about me all the time and give me care, pleasure and security, disregard all my faults and mistakes, and to be prepared to make sacrifices for me, but primarily to accept my Shame Events as their own.
Note: This is for the Unaware Mind.

I want to LOVE
Reverse of the above, with the addition of wanting to suffer for the other party's Shame Events to atone for my own.
Note: This is for the Unaware Mind.

I want to be IN LOVE
I want to love in return for being loved (see above).

I want to be LIKED
I want my Shame Events to pass unnoticed so that I can achieve a high degree of approval and acceptance.

I want to be ADMIRED
I want others to want to become part of my life at the expense of theirs. I want them to envy me and think of me as being a little mysterious.

I want to be HELD IN AWE
I want to be a mystery to others, I want them to think that my position is unattainable to them, that most of my qualities are inborn or given to me by God, and that my thinking is imperceptible to them.

I want a DISAPPOINTING LIFE
Happiness is having fucked my life up.

I want to be IMPORTANT
I want people to have fear of me so that they put my interests first, and live in accordance with my wishes.

I want to be POWERFUL
I want to be unquestionably obeyed. I want others to be so scared of me that they think that they are, or should become, my slaves.

I want to be ACKNOWLEDGED
I want to be appreciated for my skills by people of equal status with me because they understand how difficult what I do is.

I want to be CENTRE OF ATTENTION
I want to be the main object of somebody's or everybody's thinking.

I want to be FAMOUS
I want to be known by everyone.

I want to be LUCKY
I want to be favoured by fate.

I want to be RICH
I want to have so much money so as not to know what to do with it.

I want to be HEALTHY
With regard to my body, I want to have thoughts of its good health only.

I want to have a LONG LIFE
I want to live for as long as I want.

I want to be BEAUTIFUL
With regard to my beauty, I want to have peace of mind, enjoy my looks and know that others do so too.

I want to be APPRECIATED
I want people to be grateful to me for my qualities and actions, e.g. hospitality, generosity, suffering, kindness.

I want to be REMEMBERED
I want to become a frequently used memory.

I want to be CHOSEN BY GOD
I want to be special to God for my faith, suffering and sacrifices for Him, and to be his frequent object of attention.

I want to be SPECIAL
I want to be unique for being sensitive, talented, courageous etc.

I want to be RESPECTED
I want others to appreciate my superior position either because of my work or qualities, and as a result, fulfil my wishes without me having to express them.

I want to be ENVIED
I want to be hated for my qualities and/or achievements by people powerless to catch up with me or harm me.

I want to be ACCEPTED
I want to cross the threshold from a negative or non-existent relationship to a positive one.

I want to be CARED FOR
I want others to solve my problems, make my life easier, more soothing, pleasant, comfortable and secure.

I want to be THE WINNER
I want to be the first to achieve the aims that others also have.

I want to be STRONG
I want to be in complete command of my mind and body.

I want to be FREE
I want to be in command of my own destiny. I want to think what I want to think.

I want to be PERFECT
I want to take pride when comparing my body and/or my mind with the ideal.

I want to FIND OUT
I want to see the meaning of things behind their appearances or manifestations.

I want to SURVIVE
I want to stay alive. I want to get through (a period of) life unscathed.

I want to HELP PEOPLE
I want to make people think for themselves.

I want to MAKE PEOPLE HAPPY
I want to let people achieve their Purposes. I want to do what I think is best for them (and me), that is, I want people to fail.
Note: This is for the Unaware Mind.

I want to LOSE MYSELF
I want to avoid thinking painful or shameful thoughts by speeding up my thinking, or by numbing my brain with self-produced and/or introduced drugs, alcohol, food, pain, sound – even that of my own voice, self-punishment, or by making myself think pleasurable thoughts.

I want to DIE
I want to end my suffering. I want to have peace forever.

I want to HAVE PEACE OF MIND
I want to be free from thinking unpleasant thoughts.

I want to HAVE A PEACEFUL LIFE
I want to have no unexpected or unpleasant Events.

I want to BELONG
I want to be a part of someone's life
I want those with whom I and my Shame Events are safe, to be a part of my life. I want others to think that they with their Shame Events are secure with me.
(see I want to be STUPID)

I want to DO MY DUTY
I want to do a touch more than is needed to complete the task so as to have complete peace of mind.

I want to FEEL SECURE
I want to fail so as to avoid unpleasant happenings in the future.

I want to be SECURE
I want to be reassured that nothing unpleasant is going to happen.

I want to DO MY BEST
I want all my efforts, mental and physical, to be focused on what I am doing.

I want to HAVE A COMFORTABLE LIFE
I want to be able to afford all the material possessions I want.

I want to HAVE AN EASY LIFE
I want to have as few obstacles as possible and to do things with as few obstacles as possible.

I want to HAVE A FINE LIFE (To avoid thinking about my Shame Events)
I want to live among refined people and/or refined things, which are considered being especially different.

I want to HAVE A BEAUTIFUL LIFE (to avoid thinking about my Shame Events)
I want to draw enjoyment from living among beautiful things, visiting beautiful places, knowing beautiful people.

I want to HAVE A FULFILLED LIFE
I want to live my life so as to be satisfied with the way I used my time towards the fulfilment of an aware Purpose.

I want to ENJOY MY LIFE
I want to be achieving Purposes with finished thinking.

I want to ATONE
I want to be punished enough for my Shame Events to restore my peace of mind.

I want FAIRNESS (JUSTICE)
I want to be given good will for the good will that I gave first.

I want to TAKE REVENGE
I want to enjoy other people's suffering for the suffering I had (and still have) to go through.

I want to RELAX
I want to be free of mental and physical tensions.

I want to be RIGHT
I want to live as I think I should, in accordance with my visible idea of happiness.

I want to ORIENTATE MYSELF
I want to establish as many affinities as possible.

I want to be SUPERIOR
I want to know that I am above others in the qualities I use to compare. I want others to know that I am more special and important than they are.

I want to be UNDERSTOOD
I want others to know what I think and feel (even without my telling them).

I want to be ASSURED
I want to know that things are as I thought they were.

I want to SUCCEED
I want to lose myself within well-deserved or well-earned circumstances. I want to achieve what I have decided to achieve.

I want to be NEEDED
I want others to think that they will be unable to live without me, or that without me they will be unable to think the thoughts they wish they could.

I want to be INTELLIGENT
I want to know that I have knowledge to match that of other people.

I want to IMPRESS
I want others to know that I have achieved (or I can easily achieve) the high goals that I set out to achieve.

I want to UNDERSTAND
I want to create totalities from the bits of information available.

I want to be SPECIAL TO MYSELF
I want to revel or wallow in my very own thoughts and feelings (Unfinished Thinking with imagined security).

I want to be PROUD OF MYSELF
I want to take pride in succeeding where others (would have) failed.

I want an EXCITING LIFE
I want to have as many (unexpected) Events as possible. I want to lose myself in risky pleasures.

I want to FAIL
I don't want to achieve what I can.

I want to be CONFUSED
I do not want to understand what I might understand. I want to have too many, too few, or no, points of reference so as not to be able to arrive at any conclusions. I want to have a state of mind that does not allow me to understand anything.

I want to SUFFER
I want to be in (mental or physical) pain (e.g. I want to have a hard life).

I want to be LOST
I don't want to know anything. I don't want to know where I am or what I am.

I want to DESPAIR
I want to wallow in my helplessness of knowing I cannot (ever) achieve my Purpose(s).

I want to FEEL GUILTY
I want to suffer (from a gnawing feeling in my chest) because of the knowledge that I have done what I should not have done.

I want to be GUILTY
I want to do something that will make me suffer from the knowledge that I have done what I should not have done.

I want OTHERS TO FAIL
I want to prevent others from achieving what they want and can.

I want to be UNHAPPY
I don't want to enjoy what I can.

I want to be HELPLESS
I want to be unable to do what I am expected (even by myself) to do.

I want to be STUPID
I want to be unable to understand. I don't want to have clear thoughts. I don't want to know what I know. I don't want to know what the people I want to belong with don't know.

I want to be THICK
I want to be unable to see my thoughts.

I want to have a FRIGHTENING LIFE
I want to think that at any moment something terrible is going to happen, or is being prepared to happen.

I want to be REJECTED
I want others to loathe my company.

I want to PLEASE
I want to live the way I think other people want me to.

I want A WASTED LIFE
I want to spend much more time than is expedient on achieving Purposes.

I want to be UNDISCOVERED
I don't want to be found out for what I really am.

I want to be DISCOVERED
I want to be found out by others for what I really am, without my telling them.

I want to be PUNISHED
I want to have pain, physical and/or mental, inflicted on me by others for the wrongs I did.

I want to be INFERIOR
I want to know that I am worse than others.

I want to be LONELY
I want to think that I am not thought of by anyone. I want to think that there is no one with whom I can share my life.

I want to be DEPRIVED
I want fate or people in positions of power to refuse me what others get with little or no effort.

I want to FORGET
I don't want to remember my past.

I want to be HATED
I want people to loathe me or to want to beat me senseless or to want to kill me.

I want to be DESIRED
I want people to want to ravish me.

I want to be RAVISHED
I want others to gorge on me with insatiable lust.

I want to be HARD TO GET
I want others to use extra time and effort to make me belong with them.

I want to be HUMILIATED
I want others to denigrate me for my worthlessness. I want others to laugh at my failure.

I want to be SUSPECTED
I want others to think I have knowingly broken or will break a contract.

I want to be MISUNDERSTOOD
I want others to think that I am something other than what I really am. I want others to be mistaken about me.

I want to be a MYSTERY TO MYSELF
I don't want to understand myself.

I want to be STRANGE (A FUCK UP)
I want to have unconventional thinking.

I want to be MAD
I want to be unable to control my thoughts or emotions.

I want to be SEDUCED
I want to be brought to the state where I am unable, through titillation, to resist the pressure to have sex.

I want to be FUCKED
I want to be penetrated. I want to have sex.

I want to be INFLUENTIAL
I want people to change their lives as a result of them thinking about me, my words and my deeds.

I want to be UGLY
I want to be rejected as soon as I am seen.

I want to be REPULSIVE
I want others to cringe in disgust every time people look at me or think about me.

I want to be MY OWN SHAME
I want to suffer for being uniquely disgusting.

I want to be LOST IN TRIFLES
I want to be preoccupied with trivia.

I want to be FRUSTRATED
I want to be angry for having unnecessary obstacles thrown in my way by fate or by people or even myself.

I want to be TRUSTED
I want others to have complete faith in my integrity.

I want to have NO RESPONSIBILITIES
I want to blame forces outside my control for my deeds, faults and mistakes.

I want to be a BURDEN
I want to drag others down.

I want to be BETRAYED
I want my trust to be abused.

I want to be other PEOPLE'S SHAME
I want others to cringe from being associated with me.

I want to have SHAME EVENTS
I want to cringe when seeing my thoughts.

I want to be SHIT
I want to be the lowest of the low.

I want to be DISAPPOINTED
I want nobody and nothing to live up to my expectations.

I want to be NORMAL
I want to think and believe as I was meant to by nature.

I want to be FATED
I want to be incapable of controlling the events of my life.

I want to PROVOKE SUFFERING
I want to cause others (physical and/or mental) pain.

I want to be LET DOWN
I want to rely on unreliable people or things.

I want to REMEMBER
I want to keep my memories visible.

I want to be TOLD OFF
I want people to make me have to realise my mistakes.

I want to be a VICTIM OF CIRCUMSTANCES
I don't want to be responsible for my life.

I want to FEEL GOOD
I want to enjoy my physical well-being.

I want to be LOST IN SHAME
I want to be unworthy of life.

I want to be UNPREDICTABLE
I don't want to know and/or others to know what I am going to think or do next.

I want to PROVOKE ANGER
I want others to feel aggressive negative actions towards me so their Layer of Visible Thinking (pool of Awareness) shrinks and as a result (a) they are unable to think (b) they do what I want them to do.

I want to be DEVIOUS
I want to use the circumstances to my advantage.

Appendix Two
List of Actions

I accept
I accuse
I acquiesce
I admire
I admit
I agree
I allow
I apologise
I appease
I appreciate
I ask for help/ understanding
I assess
I assume
I atone
I attack
I attract attention
I avoid
I back off
I belong
I betray
I bide my time
I blackmail
I bluff
I boast
I brace myself
I bribe
I brush off
I bully
I care

I care for myself
I challenge
I clutch at straws
I compare
I complain
I condescend
I condescend to myself
I confess
I contemplate
I corner
I cover up
I cringe
I curse
I defend
I demand
I denigrate
I despair
I direct attention
I disagree
I do my best (with the Purpose I want peace of mind. The Purpose I want to be proud of myself leads to forcing, i.e. I force myself to do my best)
I do my duty
I doubt
I draw attention
I dread
I dream

I duck
I ease my way in
I encourage
I enjoy
I entice
I envy
I evade
I explain
I expose
I feed the bait
I find out
I find out about
I fish for flattery
I flatter
I flirt
I force myself
I forgive myself
I fuck myself
I give in
I give leeway
I give up
I gloat
I go limp
I gorge myself
I greet
I grieve
I grovel
I guess
I guide
I hit out
I humble myself
I humour
I hunt
I hush up
I impress
I indulge
I indulge myself

I ingratiate myself
I insist
I instruct
I joke
I jump in
I justify
I keep my fingers crossed
I keep up conversation
I kill
I kill time
I let go
I like
I long for
I look forward
I lose myself
I lure
I make peace
I memorize
I mock
I nudge
I offer help
I order
I orientate myself
I pacify
I paint a picture
I parry
I pass my time
I pass the buck
I persevere
I pity myself
I plead
I please (I want to make people happy)
I plot (a mischief)
I postpone
I pounce
I preach

I pre-empt
I preen
I prepare
I prime
I probe
I prod
I promise
I protest
I provoke anger/ attack/ interest/ regret/ remorse/ worry
I punish myself
I push
I put down
I put off
I reassure
I recall
I reflect
I regret
I regroup
I rehearse
I reject
I relax
I remember
I remind
I reproach
I rescue
I retreat
I revel
I runaway
I save face
I scold
I scream for help
I search for clues
I search my memory
I seek sympathy
I set the hook
I share

I show interest, care etc.
I shrink
I shrug off
I sneer
I snub
I soothe
I spit
I squirm
I stab (in the back)
I stand my ground
I stop
I stress
I suffer
I sulk
I survive
I suspect
I take a risk
I take my time
I take pride
I take revenge
I taunt
I tease
I tell off
I terminate
I test
I threaten
I torture
I trap
I triumph
I wait
I want to be liked, accepted, appreciated
I want to lose myself
I warn
I whip
I wish
I worry

Glossary

ACCUMULATED EVENT
An Event unnoticeably created over a long period of time from a series of unimportant thoughts

ACTIONS
What I do to achieve my Purpose

AFFINITIES
Every activated thought in a Complex other than the main one

AFTERBURN
Aware Dissipation

ANTICIPATION
Increasing intensity of thinking in imaginary pictures and impressions

AWARENESS
The ability to see one's own thinking

BODYGUARDS
Thoughts, impressions and sensations designed to keep me in my Mind Erosion

CIRCUMSTANCES
Mundane Happenings

COGS
The process of imposing thinking on others
or
The Mind Balance* (developing or set) between two people
*see separate definition

COMPLEX
An interconnected group of thoughts where when one is activated then so are the others to different degrees

CONSCIOUSNESS
An ever-changing totality of thoughts and neurobiological processes
or
A Super Complex of Complexes

DEVICES
What I want others to think I do

EMERGING AWARENESS
The first perceived and most remembered episodes from one's life

EVENT
Intensified thinking itself

FOREBURN
Aware Anticipation

FINISHING-OFF THINKING
Taking thoughts beyond the point where they were interrupted by fear

GO LIMP
To physically and mentally relax on a thought(s)

GHOST
A recurring fear that has the Purpose of maintaining an unawarely favoured pattern of thinking/behaviour.

HAPPENING
A change in the physical world

IMPORTANT THOUGHTS
Thoughts that think themselves irrespective of the circumstances

LIFE SITUATION
A set of circumstances that set a precedent for future Events and behaviours, regardless of the context and relevancy

MIND BALANCE
The relationship between two or more people

MIND EROSION
Paths or patterns of thinking followed irrespective of the visible circumstances

MINDPRINT
A verbal embodiment of the elements of the mind and its important, generalised and invisible thoughts.
(Important, because they think themselves irrespective of circumstances. Generalised, because they are summaries of past experiences that are used as points of reference for experiences that are happening or are as yet to happen. Invisible, because we do not see them)

MINDQUAKE
An Event which requires considerably more thinking effort to process than most Events

NATURAL FRAME OF REFERENCE
Purposes and other points of reference necessary for life

PURPOSE
What I think will make me happy

SHAME EVENTS
The thoughts that cause me the most suffering and the ones that I must hide from others as well as myself

ULTIMATE COMMUNION EVENT
A generalized impression of the most secure relationship I could ever be in

UNFINISHED THINKING
Thoughts interrupted by fear

Notes and References

Chapter 3 – Complexes
1. B.Libet, *Neurophysiology of Consciousness* Springer Science and Business Media, 1993, p269-306
2. E. Berne, *What Do You Say After You Say Hello?* London: Corgi, 1988, p31

Chapter 5 – Formation of Consciousness
3. J. Fallon, *The Psychopath Inside: A Neuroscientist's Personal Journey into the Dark Side of the Brain* New York: Penguin, 2015

Chapter 6 – Mindprint
4. *Heauton Timorumenos* (*The Self-Tormentor*) is a play written by Publius Terentius Afer, known in English as "Terence", a dramatist of the Roman Republic. The original quote reads *"Homo sum, humani nihil a me alienum puto"*, or "I am human, and nothing of that which is human is alien to me."
5. T. Williams, *Orpheus Descending* (Act 2, Scene 1): Dramatists Play Service 1983

Chapter 8 – Finishing off Thinking
6. M. Aurelius, *The Thoughts of the Emperor Marcus Aurelius Antoninus*, trans. G. Long, Whitefish, MT:Kessinger, 2004, pp1-3
7. E Jong, *How to Save Your Own Life*, New York: Penguin 2006

Chapter 9 – FoffTing Questions and Tools
8. See http://quoteinvestigator.com/2014/09/04/truth-free/

Final Guiding Words
9. Earliest occurrence available online: "William James wrote that a great many people think they are thinking when they are merely rearranging their

prejudices." in: *Trust Management Update* (1983), Issues 63–80, page civ. Omnipaedista (talk) 19:45, 20 May 2014 (UTC)

Workshops

If you are interested in finding out more about this work or would like to
attend one of the regularly held workshops, please see
www.whywethinkthewaywedo.com for details.